Drive and Stroll i

Cambridgeshire

●

Martin Hall

COUNTRYSIDE BOOKS
NEWBURY BERKSHIRE

First published 2007
© Martin Hall 2007

COUNTRYSIDE BOOKS
3 Catherine Road
Newbury, Berkshire

To view our complete range of books,
please visit us at
www.countrysidebooks.co.uk

ISBN 978 1 85306 957 4

Cover picture of the River Ouse at St Ives supplied by
Pictures of Britain (Adam Swaine)

Photographs by the author
Maps by Gelder Design & Mapping

Designed by Peter Davies, Nautilus Design
Produced through MRM Associates Ltd., Reading
Typeset by Jean Cussons Typesetting, Diss, Norfolk
Printed by Borcombe SP Ltd., Romsey

Contents

Introduction 6

Walk 1   Maxey (2½ miles) 7

Walk 2   Parson Drove (2½ miles) 11

Walk 3   Castor (2½ miles) 16

Walk 4   Yaxley (2¾ miles) 20

Walk 5   Whittlesey (5 miles) 25

Walk 6   Benwick (3½ miles) 29

Walk 7   Ouse Washes Nature Reserve (4 miles) 33

Walk 8   Abbots Ripton (3 miles) 37

Walk 9   Prickwillow (5 miles) 41

Walk 10   Catworth (3¼ miles) 45

Walk 11   Grafham Water (4½ miles) 49

Walk 12   Fen Drayton (5 miles) 54

Walk 13   Aldreth (4¼ miles) 59

Walk 14   Wicken Fen (4¼ miles) 64

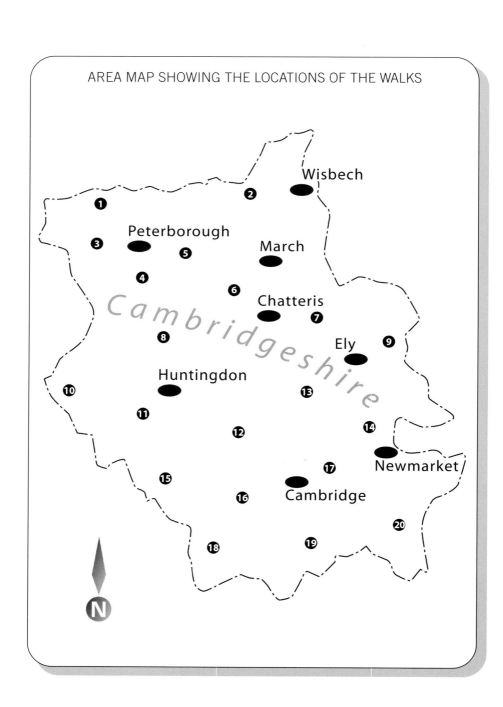

AREA MAP SHOWING THE LOCATIONS OF THE WALKS

Contents

Walk 15	Abbotsley (4 miles)	69
Walk 16	Great Eversden (4 miles)	74
Walk 17	Lode (3½ miles)	78
Walk 18	Abington Pigotts (3¾ miles)	82
Walk 19	Hinxton (3 miles)	87
Walk 20	Horseheath (3½ miles)	92

PUBLISHER'S NOTE

We hope that you obtain considerable enjoyment from this book; great care has been taken in its preparation. Although at the time of publication all routes followed public rights of way or permitted paths, diversion orders can be made and permissions withdrawn.

We cannot, of course, be held responsible for such diversion orders and any inaccuracies in the text which result from these or any other changes to the routes nor any damage which might result from walkers trespassing on private property. We are anxious though that all details covering the walks are kept up to date and would therefore welcome information from readers which would be relevant to future editions.

The simple sketch maps that accompany the walks in this book are based on notes made by the author whilst checking the routes on the ground. However, for the benefit of a proper map, we do recommend that you purchase the relevant Ordnance Survey sheet covering your walk. The Ordnance Survey maps are widely available, especially through booksellers and local newsagents.

Introduction

Cambridgeshire is an attractive and historic county, full of surprises. There are beautiful rivers, quiet country lanes, open meadows, picture-postcard villages, nature reserves, ancient buildings and modern cities, all packed into an area of around 1,300 square miles. The county is perhaps best known for its fens – a complex system of dykes and waterways, used to control flooding. This work was first carried out by the Romans, but was later improved upon by Dutch engineers, during the 17th century.

The Romans left a rich legacy, and new discoveries continue to be made to this day. The walk at Castor allows you to step back to this time, for the village started life as a suburban area of a Roman market town known as Durobrivae – centre of the Roman pottery industry in Britain. It was also the site of one of the largest Roman villas found in the country.

There are plenty of other treasures to unearth as you walk your way through the book – such as the beautifully restored watermills, which can be found at Lode and Hinxton; the historic and entertaining Straw Bear Festival at Whittlesey; the National Trust's oldest nature reserve at Wicken Fen; and the walk around the village of Aldreth, which was the site of violent clashes between William the Conqueror and legendary Saxon leader, Hereward the Wake. A close encounter with nature, or sweeping views across a scenic landscape can enhance the enjoyment of a walk in the countryside, and the routes in this book were designed with this in mind.

The 20 circular routes take advantage of the county's network of over 2,000 miles of public rights of way. The walks vary in length between 2½ and 5 miles, and have been devised to provide enjoyment and entertainment for all. Details of pubs, restaurants or cafés which can be found along the course of each route, or close by, are included. For those wishing to turn their walk into a full-day event, local attractions, such as country houses, museums and zoos are also listed.

A sketch map is provided for each walk to serve as a rough guide. However, I strongly recommend that you carry with you the relevant Ordnance Survey map, as they are invaluable for highlighting detail and also allow you to extend the suggested route, if required. I have given the appropriate Landranger sheet number and title for each. Despite the easy terrain, I would also recommend wearing walking boots, and a small backpack can be useful for carrying drinks and snacks.

Finally, I hope that the routes in this book will provide you with many happy hours of walking in this wonderful county.

Martin Hall

1 | Maxey

Maxey Cut

The Walk 2½ miles ⊕ 1¼ hours
Map OS Landranger 142 Peterborough (GR 130081)

How to get there

From Peterborough, head north on the A15 towards Market Deeping. At a traffic island, where the B1524 and the B1162 branch off from the A15, turn left along an unclassified road, which brings you into Maxey. **Parking:** Roadside parking is available on High Street, close to the Blue Bell pub. Patrons may use their car park, but a gate is often shut when the pub is closed.

Drive and Stroll

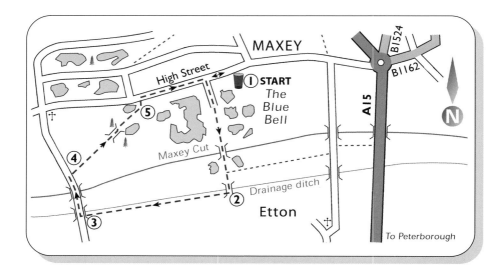

Introduction

This relaxing walk begins in the ancient village of Maxey, which is situated a short distance to the south of the River Welland. It was first recorded in the Anglo-Saxon Chronicles in 1013, when it was spelt Makesey. However, archaeological excavation suggests that the area has been inhabited for around 4,000 years. After passing attractive lakes, you cross a bridge that spans Maxey Cut – a scenic stretch of water which forms part of the surrounding fenland drainage system, and which diverts flood water away from the town of Market Deeping. Later, you encounter country lanes and open farmland, before walking through the village and back to the starting point.

Refreshments

The **Blue Bell**, at the start of the walk, is an attractive pub, with beamed ceilings and stone floors. Real ales are available and sandwiches can be arranged for groups of walkers, provided that they are requested a few hours beforehand. Open seven days a week (evenings only on Monday to Friday). Telephone: 01778 348182. Alternatively, try the **Golden Pheasant** at Etton, located about 2 miles to the south-east of Maxey. Real ales and a wide choice of good quality food are available, and there is a beer garden and children's play area. Open every day except Monday. Telephone: 01733 252387.

Grey heron frequent the waters around Maxey

THE WALK

 (1)

With the main door of the **Blue Bell** behind you, bear left and walk along the pavement, passing picture-postcard cottages as you go. After about 70 yards, turn left along **Woodgate Lane**, passing houses on either side. A little further on, the well-surfaced lane becomes a wide, stony track. Continue ahead, as you pass a series of attractive lakes on either side. These are former gravel pit workings, which are now used by anglers. They are also a good place to see a variety of water birds. Further on, cross a bridge over **Maxey Cut**, from where there are fine views along its length. Keep straight ahead, passing more gravel pits to your left and right and then continue until you reach a wooden footbridge.

 (2)

Cross the bridge, then turn right and walk along a grassy footpath with a narrow drainage ditch to your right,

9

and an even narrower one to the left. As you walk, look out for skylarks singing above the fields and herons hunting beside the ditches. Continue straight ahead until you arrive at a lane.

Turn right along the lane and cross a road bridge, which spans the drainage ditch you have just been walking beside. As you continue, look out for any oncoming traffic. Further on, cross a road bridge over **Maxey Cut**, with views along the water. Carry on along the lane and, immediately after passing a small brick farm building, you reach a signed footpath on your right-hand side.

Bear diagonally right here and follow the path which runs beside a line of telegraph poles. At the far side of a field, the line of telegraph poles veers off to the right. At this point, continue in the same direction as

before and, at the far side of a field, cross a footbridge over a drainage ditch. Turn left immediately after crossing the bridge and then veer right to walk through a lightly wooded area. Continue along a well-trodden path, keeping a small fishing lake to your right. After passing to the side of a metal gate, you reach a stony track. Turn left here and, soon, the track becomes a well-surfaced lane. Pass a house and another fishing lake to your left, before passing to the side of a decorative metal gate. Continue ahead to reach a road.

Turn right and pass houses on either side. A little further on, you pass a beautiful thatched cottage on your left-hand side. Follow the road, as it curves to the left slightly, then pass **Woodgate Lane** on your right. Ahead of you is the **Blue Bell** pub, which brings the walk to an end.

Place of Interest Nearby

Tallington Lakes Leisure Park is situated 3 miles to the north-west of Maxey. It offers 205 acres of water, providing windsurfing, water-skiing, canoeing, sailing and fishing. There are also landscaped areas, an adventure playground and camping and caravanning facilities, while refreshments are provided in the on-site bar and restaurant. The park and facilities are open all year round, except for the camping and caravanning amenities, which are closed during February. Telephone: 01778 347000.

2 Parson Drove

The Cage, near the start of the route, was built in 1829, and was once used as a fire station

The Walk 2½ miles 🕐 1¼ hours
Map OS Landranger 142 Peterborough (GR 371084)

How to get there

From March, head north on the A141. After 3½ miles, turn left along the A47 and, after a few hundred yards, turn right and follow the B1187 for 3¾ miles, to arrive at the village of Parson Drove. **Parking**: Patrons may use the Swan Inn car park, otherwise park on Main Road (B1166) close by.

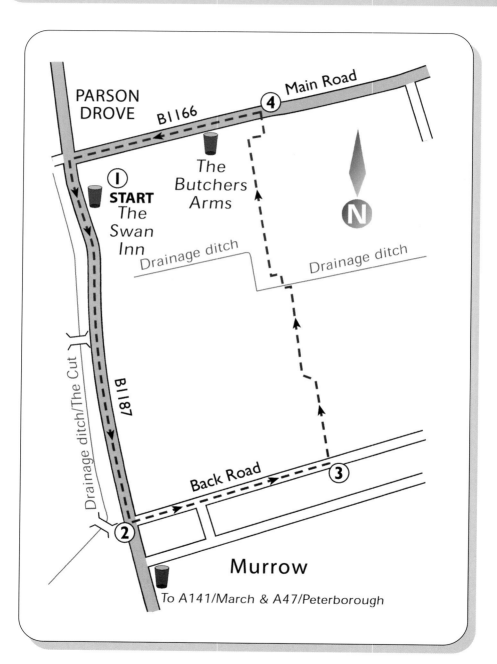

Introduction

Parson Drove is an attractive village, located less than a mile away from the Lincolnshire county border. This short, but enjoyable, route leads you along country roads and open farmland crossed with ditches and dykes. Starting at the Swan Inn, you immediately pass a curious little building known affectionately as The Cage. Built in 1829 by a local constable named John Peck, it provides a physical link with the history of the village. During its time, it has served as an overnight lock-up for minor law breakers, a pen for stray animals, a fire station and a wartime police post. These days, however, it is an Interpretation Centre, telling the history of the village through books and photographs. It is open to the public on Wednesday and Sunday afternoons from April to September. The large clock tower on the roof of the building was added in 1897, to celebrate Queen Victoria's Diamond Jubilee.

Refreshments

The **Swan Inn**, dating back to around 1580, was visited by Samuel Pepys, who lodged there for a night in 1663. It serves real ales and bar snacks such as ploughman's lunches, pizzas and sausages and mash. Open throughout the week (evenings only on Monday to Friday). Telephone: 01945 700291. Alternatively, the **Butchers Arms** restaurant and bar is passed near the end of the route. Open from Tuesday to Sunday, it serves snacks such as sandwiches, through to main meals like steak, lasagne and fish dishes. Telephone: 01945 700232.

THE WALK

(1)

With the **Swan Inn** behind you, aim slightly left to walk through the car park and then continue to **The Cage**, which you may wish to enter during open afternoons. Pass the building on your left-hand side and then turn left to walk on the pavement along **Station Road** (B1187). After passing houses to your left, the pavement runs out. Cross the road at this point and then turn left to continue along the roadside, looking out for any oncoming traffic. To your right is a wide dyke, known as **The Cut**. As you walk, there are some fine views across the farmland to your left. Further on, a bridleway crosses a footbridge over the dyke, immediately to your right. Continue ahead on the road, where you will see a road sign announcing the village of **Murrow**.

 (2)

Soon after passing this, turn left to walk along **Back Road**. A little

Drive and Stroll

Open fields are a feature of this walk

further on, ignore a lane off to the right, but continue straight ahead, passing attractive houses on either side. Keep walking straight on until you come to a signed footpath on your left-hand side.

  ③

Turn left here and follow the well-trodden path straight ahead. As you pass fields on either side, you may see skylarks overhead. After about 150 yards, a white arrow on a

marker post guides you to the left. After 40 yards, follow another white arrow, which guides you to the right, then continue straight ahead along the edge of a field, keeping a ditch to your right. After about 550 yards, follow a white arrow on a marker post, which guides you to the left. Turn right after 40 yards to cross a drainage ditch, then turn immediately left. Continue for 20 yards, then turn right to follow another white arrow. Walk straight ahead, keeping a drainage ditch to your left. A little further on, the drainage ditch curves off to the left. Continue straight ahead at this point, with open fields on either side of you. Pass houses on your left-hand side, then turn right to follow a marker post. Pass an old barn on your left and then turn left. Pass a house on your right-hand side to reach a road.

 (4)

Cross the road and then turn left to walk along the pavement, passing some beautiful houses as you go. Over to your left is the **Butchers Arms** if you wish to call in for refreshment. Otherwise, keep going straight ahead until you arrive back at the **Swan Inn**, which can be seen to your left.

Places of Interest Nearby

Peckover House and Garden (National Trust) is located at Wisbech, 6¼ miles to the north-east of Parson Drove. The house dates back to around 1722, and is known for its fine plaster and wood rococo decoration, while the garden includes an orangery, roses and croquet lawn. Open on Tuesday, Wednesday, Saturday and Sunday from March to November. Also open on Bank Holiday Monday. Telephone: 01945 583463.

Wisbech & Fenland Museum, also located at Wisbech, is said to be the oldest purpose-built museum in the country. The present building dates back to 1847. Inside are a fenland exhibition, coins, medals, photographs, artworks and natural history exhibits. The museum also holds the original manuscript of Dickens' *Great Expectations*, which can be viewed by the public on the first Saturday of each month. Telephone: 01945 583817.

3 Castor

The River Nene

The Walk 2½ miles 🕐 1½ hours
Map OS Landranger 142 Peterborough (GR 123984)

How to get there

Castor is located 2½ miles west of Peterborough, and is sandwiched between the A47 and the A1. **Parking**: On Peterborough Road, beside the village hall, or close by.

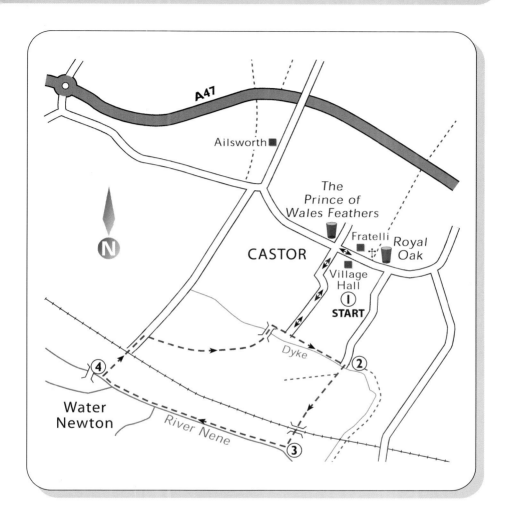

Introduction

Despite its relatively close proximity to the city of Peterborough, Castor has a truly rural feel to it. The attractive thatched cottages and stone houses hide an intriguing history, for the village started life as a suburban area of a thriving Roman market town known as Durobrivae – centre of the Roman pottery industry. One of its main exports was 'Castorware', which has since been found as far away as Turkey. Castor was also the site of one of the largest Roman villas in Britain. Later, the Normans, too, made an impression, as can be seen from the stunning architecture of St Kyneburgha's church. Soon after leaving the village, this enjoyable route takes you beside the banks of the River Nene, and then onwards through beautiful water meadows rich in wild flowers, before curving back round to cross the Nene Valley Railway and the course of an ancient Roman road.

Refreshments

The **Fratelli Restaurant** is a traditional Italian restaurant (the old Fitzwilliam Arms) and can be found opposite the village hall. It serves food seven days a week. Telephone: 01733 380251.

There are also two good pubs in the village – the **Prince of Wales Feathers** offers a wide choice of lunches from a regularly changing menu. Hours may vary. Telephone: 01733 380222. The **Royal Oak** offers light lunches and quality real ale. It also has an attractive front patio garden. Telephone: 01733 380217.

THE WALK

With the village hall immediately to your left, and the **Fratelli Restaurant** to your right, walk straight ahead along the pavement, passing delightful cottages as you go. At a crossroads, you will see the **Prince of Wales Feathers** pub to your right. Turn left along **Port Lane**. The well-surfaced road becomes a stony track, as you bear left, then immediately right. Pass a large sports ground on your left, then a cricket pitch on your right, to arrive at a junction of tracks. Turn left along a well-trodden path, keeping a narrow dyke to your right. Follow the path as it curves gently to the right. Pass a stone footbridge on your right and continue. The path

then bends slightly left, bringing you to a wide track.

Turn sharp right and cross a footbridge over the dyke, then walk ahead, keeping a line of trees to your left. There are some fine open views across the fields to your right. Walk under a bridge, which carries the **Nene Valley Railway** overhead, then cross a stile and continue ahead until you reach the **River Nene**.

On the opposite side of the river, and slightly to your left, is where the Roman town of Durobrivae once stood. Turn right along a well-used path, keeping the river immediately to your left. Further on, go over a stile and then cross a wooden bridge, before continuing ahead through scenic water meadows. After about 100 yards, a backwater branches off from the river and meanders its way towards the village of **Water Newton**, with its 18th-century watermill just visible from the footpath. Keep straight ahead, still with the river to your left. Cross a stile and a footbridge and walk on to a gate, which is situated close to a bridge spanning the river.

 (4)

Do not go through the gate, but instead, turn right along a well-trodden path, keeping a hedge to your left. Cross the **Nene Valley Railway** (look out for steam trains chugging past) and then continue ahead on a narrow lane. After a few yards, turn

right along a signed footpath. This curves slightly to the left after about 200 yards, taking you across the course of an old Roman road called **Ermine Street** – although nothing can be seen of it from ground level. Go through a gap in the hedge and follow the path, which, at this point, is a slightly raised bank running across a field. At the far side of the field, cross a footbridge over a dyke and then turn right. Continue for about 50 yards, to reach the junction of tracks encountered near the start of the route. Turn left and pass the cricket pitch and sports ground, then retrace your steps back along **Port Lane**. Turn right along **Peterborough Road** and walk back to the starting point.

Places of Interest Nearby

The **Nene Valley Railway's** headquarters are at Wansford station, a short distance west of Castor. Traditional steam and diesel trains run throughout the year, between Yarwell Junction and Peterborough. Their 'Thomas' engine is especially popular with children. Telephone: 01780 784444 for details.

Ferry Meadows Country Park, to the east of Castor, is the centrepiece of Nene Park Trust. There are scenic lakes, nature trails, a visitor centre, café and birdwatching hides. Telephone: 01733 234443.

4 Yaxley

The countryside around Yaxley

The Walk 2¾ miles ⓡ 1½ hours
Map OS Landranger 142 Peterborough (GR 189922)

How to get there

From the southern edge of Peterborough, drive south for 2½ miles on the B1091, which brings you into Yaxley. **Parking**: Park on Main Street, near the Duck and Drake pub. Patrons may use their car park.

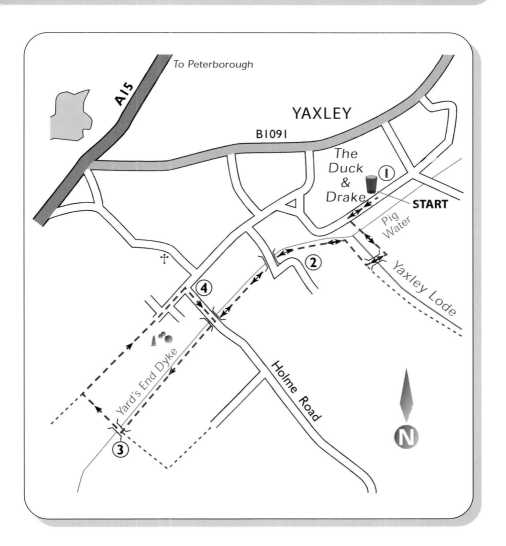

Introduction

Yaxley is mentioned in the Domesday Book and, since that time, has grown and developed into a thriving community. This route starts in the lower part of the village, which is also the oldest. Before the fens were drained, it served as an inland port to boats sailing on Whittlesey Mere. During the Napoleonic Wars, prisoners were shipped to Yaxley, before being transported to a camp at the nearby village of Norman Cross. After crossing a bridge over Yaxley Lode, you trace the route of Yard's End Dyke and then continue through fields and along lanes, from where the ornate and impressive St Peter's church can be seen. The return leg of the journey takes you back beside the water to the starting point.

Refreshments

The **Duck and Drake**, at the start of the walk, incorporates an Indian restaurant which also serves a small number of English dishes. Open seven days a week. Telephone: 01733 240476. Alternatively, the **Three Horseshoes**, also on Main Street, serves a wide variety of more traditional pub food. Open all week. Telephone: 01733 242059. Or try **Antonino's Pizza House**, again on Main Street, for Italian pizza and pasta. Hours may vary. Telephone: 01733 243197.

THE WALK

From the roadside, walk towards the **Duck and Drake** pub and pass it on your right-hand side. A little further on, turn left and follow a signed footpath, passing a house on your right. Follow the path, as it bends to the right and then the left, before continuing ahead. Turn right to cross a footbridge over **Yaxley Lode** – an attractive stretch of water used for drainage and boating – and then turn right again. For a short distance, the lode accompanies you to your right, before the path curves to the left and leads you along the course of **Yard's End Dyke**, which can now be seen to your right. Walk ahead on the grassy path, passing houses over to your right and open fields to your left. Further on, the path curves to the right slightly and you pass a house on your left-hand side, before reaching a bend in a road.

Walk ahead along the road and, where it bends to the right, go straight ahead along a signed footpath, still with the dyke to your right. Pass the grounds of **Yaxley Football Club** on your left-hand side and then continue ahead. After passing allotments to your left, there are good views across open fields. Further on, cross a road and continue in the same direction as before, following the course of the dyke. Keep going until you reach a stony track, which runs from left to right.

Turn right here and follow the path

Yaxley Lode

as it takes you over **Yard's End Dyke**. Pass a hedge to your left and fields to the right and then continue to a junction of unmarked paths. Turn right and then carry on along the wide, grassy path, with fields on either side of you. Further on, ignore an unmarked path to the right, but keep straight ahead, passing a field to your left and trees to your right. The beautiful spire of **St Peter's church** can be seen to your half-left. Where the grassy path becomes a stony track, keep going straight on. Pass between two metal gates and walk ahead along a residential

Drive and Stroll

road. Pass **Cookson Close** on the right and continue to a sharp bend in the road.

At this point, turn right along **Holme Road**, paying careful attention to any oncoming traffic. Soon after passing a small cluster of office and industrial units, cross a road bridge over **Yard's End Dyke**. Immediately after going over the bridge, turn left along the signed footpath encountered earlier on the walk. Continue ahead on the grassy path, this time with the dyke to your left. Further on, pass **Yaxley Football Club** on your right and then walk straight ahead along the road used before. Where the road bends to the right, go straight on along the signed footpath. Continue, with the dyke to your left and, eventually, cross the footbridge over **Yaxley Lode** once more. Turn left after going over the bridge and then follow the path back to the road. Turn right along the road and walk the short distance back to the starting point, beside the **Duck and Drake** pub.

Places of Interest Nearby

Elton Hall is set in beautiful parkland and is located 6 miles to the west of Yaxley. This fine house is built in a mixture of styles, and the south front incorporates a 15th-century tower. There are paintings by Constable, Reynolds and Gainsborough, fine furniture and an impressive library, which includes Henry VIII's prayer book. Open throughout the summer. Telephone: 01832 280468.

The historic city of **Peterborough**, a few miles to the north of Yaxley, is also worth a visit. It boasts an impressive Norman cathedral, museums, theatres, cinemas and a wide choice of pubs and restaurants.

5 | Whittlesey

Walking beside Whittlesey Dyke

The Walk 5 miles ⏱ 2½ hours
Map OS Landranger 142 Peterborough (GR 281958)

How to get there

From Peterborough, head east on the A605 for 4½ miles. In the centre of Whittlesey, follow the B1093 for a mile, then branch off to the right along an unclassified road signed to Ramsey. **Parking**: Park on the grass verge by the roadside, about 100 yards after leaving the B1093. Take care not to obstruct driveways.

Drive and Stroll

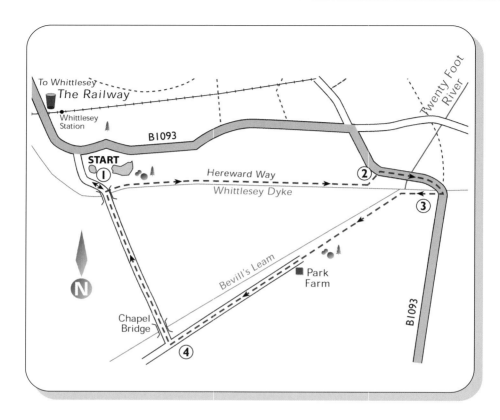

Introduction

This scenic waterside walk starts on the edge of Whittlesey – an historic market town with a 17th-century butter cross and well-preserved architecture spanning hundreds of years. It is perhaps best known for its Straw Bear Festival, which takes place each January. In this ancient agricultural custom, two or more men are 'dorned out', or dressed, in straw. A head is added and loosely fashioned to resemble a bear, and the 'Straw Bears' are then led through the streets, followed by a procession of dancers, musicians and entertainers. Whittlesey is one of the few places in the country where this tradition is still observed. The route takes you along the Hereward Way beside Whittlesey Dyke, and over a bridge spanning the Twenty Foot River. You then walk beside Bevill's Leam. All three stretches of water form an important part of the fenland drainage structure. A country lane then leads you back to the starting point.

Refreshments

The nearest pub is the **Railway**, on Station Road (close to Whittlesey train station). A selection of bar snacks is available as well as more substantial evening meals. Open evenings only on Monday to Friday, all day on Saturday and Sunday. Telephone: 01733 203232. Alternatively, there is a wide choice of pubs, restaurants and takeaways in the town centre.

THE WALK

①

With the B1093 behind you, walk ahead along the roadside and follow it as it curves to the left slightly. Soon, it bends to the right, bringing you to a road bridge spanning **Whittlesey Dyke**. To the right is a well-preserved Second World War gun emplacement, or 'pillbox'. Do not cross the bridge, but turn left along a signed footpath (the **Hereward Way**). On reaching the edge of a field, walk straight ahead, passing a fishing lake over to your left and with a hedge to your right. Climb over a stile at the far side of the field and carry on ahead. Cross another stile at the end of the next field and continue. Cross a third stile and then walk ahead on a wide, grassy path, keeping **Whittlesey Dyke** to your right and fields to your left. Pass farm buildings on the opposite side of the dyke and enjoy the views as you walk. Further on, pass farm buildings to your left and keep going until you reach a bend in the road.

②

At this point, leave the grassy bank and follow the **Hereward Way** as it continues along the B1093. Stay alert to any traffic as you go and, a little further on, cross a road bridge at a confluence of waterways. To the left is the **Twenty Foot River** and to the right is **Bevill's Leam**, while **Whittlesey Dyke** continues ahead. As you approach the next bridge, you may wish to cross to the left-hand side of the road, in order to keep a clear view of oncoming traffic. Once across the bridge, you arrive at a signed footpath on your right.

③

Follow the path along the bank of **Whittlesey Dyke** and, as you reach a stone triangulation pillar on your left, you will see the confluence of waterways again. Follow the path round to the left, now with **Bevill's Leam** on your right-hand side. As you walk, there are good views down this long straight stretch of water. Further down the grassy path, you pass a stand of trees to your left. Soon after, walk through a gap in a wooden fence and then

Drive and Stroll

pass **Park Farm** on your left-hand side. Continue ahead on a well-surfaced lane, still with **Bevill's Leam** to your right. After passing a cottage and farm buildings to your left, you reach a sharp bend in the road.

  (4)

Turn right along the road and cross **Chapel Bridge**, which spans **Bevill's Leam**. Keep going along the road, passing houses and farm buildings to your left and right. As you walk, there are open fields on either side of you, and drainage ditches running away from the roadside. Further on, cross a road bridge over **Whittlesey Dyke**. Pass the footpath used near the start of the walk and pass the gun emplacement to your left. Follow the road round, keeping the dyke to your left. Retrace your earlier steps along the road and back to the starting point.

Place of Interest Nearby

Whittlesey Museum is housed in the 19th-century town hall, on Market Street. Opened in 1976, it tells the agricultural and social history of Whittlesey and the surrounding area. Exhibits include archaeology, costumes, photographs, toys, archives and the tusk of a woolly mammoth. Open all year round from 2.30 pm to 4.30 pm on Friday and Sunday, and 10 am to 12 noon on Saturday. Open at other times by appointment. Telephone: 01733 840968.

6 Benwick

The River Nene, where you may spot a kingfisher or heron as you stroll along

The Walk 3½ miles 🕐 1¾ hours
Map OS Landranger 142 Peterborough (GR 341904)

How to get there

From Ramsey, drive north-east for 5½ miles on the B1096, which brings you into the village centre. **Parking**: Park on High Street (B1096), just to the south of a sharp bend in the road.

Drive and Stroll

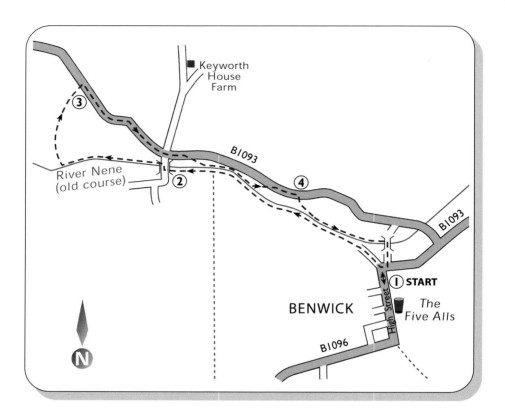

Introduction

Situated approximately midway between the market towns of Ramsey and March, Benwick is a peaceful fenland village on the banks of the River Nene (old course). According to ancient folklore, a seer and healer thought to have been named Mary, lived in the vicinity in the 14th century. It is said that despite curing the villagers of various ills, she herself died at a young age and, upon her death, the river became magical and the community was blessed with the gift of foresight. She was later branded as a witch, however, and from that point, she became known as Gresalda.

This route takes you beside the river and, although I cannot guarantee that you will obtain strange new powers, or witness magical events, I can assure you that you will encounter some beautiful scenery along the way, and perhaps catch a glimpse of a kingfisher or grey heron, as you stroll along the banks.

Refreshments

The **Five Alls** pub can be found on High Street, a short distance from the starting point. A picture on the wall explains how it came by its unusual name. A wide choice of food is available from snacks through to main meals. Opening times may vary. Telephone: 01354 677520.

THE WALK

Head roughly north on **High Street** and, where **Doddington Road** bends sharply to the right, continue straight ahead. Just before reaching a small patch of grass, veer round to the left and walk along a well-surfaced track. Continue ahead, keeping the **River Nene** (old course) to your right. A little further on, the well-surfaced track becomes a grassy path. Carry on along the riverbank, with fields to your left. Follow the path as it meanders beside the river and, as you continue, good views open out across the landscape. Keep going until you reach a narrow track beside a bridge.

Turn right and cross the bridge over the river to reach a road (**B1093**). Turn left along the road and after a few steps turn left to follow a signed footpath. On reaching the riverbank, turn right and continue along a grassy path, this time with the river to your left. Pass farm buildings over to your left and open fields to your right. This stretch of the river is a good place to see kingfishers, herons and other water birds. Further on, the river begins to bend to the left. At this point, turn right to follow a marker post. Continue on a grassy path and pass farm buildings to your left. Soon after, the grassy path meets a stony track. Continue ahead on the track, as you walk between two fields. Hares can sometimes be seen at the side of the track. Further on, the track becomes a well-surfaced lane, as it curves gently to the right and leads you past houses on your left-hand side. Continue to a road (**B1093**).

Turn right along the road, paying careful attention to any oncoming traffic as you go. Keep going along the road as it curves first to the left and then the right. As you reach a narrow road off to the left, you will see the bridge used earlier to your right. Do not cross the bridge this time, but walk along the adjacent grassy bank, keeping the river immediately to your right and the road to your left. After a while, you will see a road sign marked '**Benwick**'. Leave the grassy path soon after and continue along the

Drive and Stroll

pavement beside the road. Immediately after passing a house on the right, you arrive at a signed footpath.

 4

Turn right here and pass the house on your right-hand side. Follow the path as it then curves to the left, taking you past a house on your left. Continue ahead on the well-surfaced path, keeping the river to your right. Further on, you pass gardens and houses to your left. Soon after passing a cemetery on your left-hand side, you reach a narrow lane. Turn right here and cross a footbridge over the river. Pass a path to your right, which was used at the beginning of the walk, and continue ahead to complete the route.

Places of Interest Nearby

Ramsey Rural Museum can be found at Ramsey, 5½ miles to the south-west of Benwick. Housed in 17th-century farm buildings and set in open countryside, it tells the story of fenland life throughout history. There are various displays and exhibits, as well as local and family history archives. Disabled access and facilities are also available. Open on Thursday, Sunday and Bank Holiday Monday from April to September. Telephone: 01487 814304 or 01487 815715.

    Ramsey Abbey Gatehouse (National Trust) is also located at Ramsey. Fragments of a former Benedictine abbey can be seen, including a lavishly carved, late 15th-century gatehouse, complete with ornate oriel window. The exterior can be viewed all year, but interior access is limited. Telephone: 01480 301494.

7 | Ouse Washes Nature Reserve

The grassy track at the edge of the nature reserve at the start of the walk

The Walk 4 miles ⓘ 2 hours
Map OS Landranger 143 Ely & Wisbech (GR 471860)

How to get there

From the centre of Chatteris, head east on the B1098. After 2 miles, turn right along an unclassified road towards Manea, then turn right again after 3 miles and follow signs to the reserve and Purls Bridge. Pass the Ship Inn on your right and continue ahead to the car park. **Parking**: Use the reserve car park at Welches Dam. Donations are welcomed.

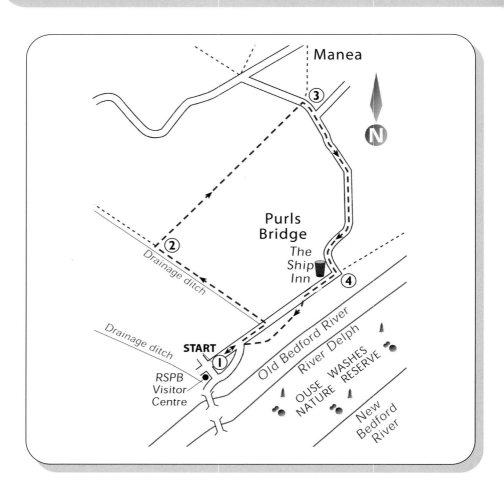

Introduction

Ouse Washes Nature Reserve is owned jointly by the RSPB and the Wildlife Trust for Bedfordshire, Cambridgeshire, Northamptonshire and Peterborough. It is set in rural fenland countryside and covers more than 3,000 acres of grass fields or 'washes', which are sandwiched between the Old Bedford River and the New Bedford River. In winter the fields flood, attracting thousands of wildfowl to the reserve. The water drains away in spring and draws other birds to the area, where a variety of insects and wild flowers also flourish. After leaving the reserve car park, you walk over open fields and beside a traditional drainage ditch. A wide track then leads you to a country road, which takes you to Purls Bridge. The final stretch of the route is along the scenic Old Bedford River, where you may see swans, ducks, or a colourful kingfisher. Back at the car park, you may wish to call in at the informative visitor centre, or visit one of the ten birdwatching hides located along the riverbank.

Refreshments

The **Ship Inn** at Purls Bridge is passed on the route. A wide choice of food is available, together with a selection of real ales. Open evenings only on Monday to Saturday, and all day on Sunday. Food is served on Friday and Saturday evenings, and on Sunday afternoons. Telephone: 01354 680578.

Alternatively, Chatteris is located 5 miles to the west of the reserve and has a broad range of pubs and restaurants, including the **Cross Keys Hotel** on Market Hill. They serve morning coffee, lunch and dinner throughout the week. Telephone: 01354 693036.

THE WALK

Leave the reserve car park and walk along the road, keeping the grassy banks of the **Old Bedford River** to your right. A little further on, turn left to follow a signed bridleway and then continue ahead, with a drainage ditch immediately to your left. As you walk, smaller drainage ditches branch off to the left and right. Keep going along the grassy path until you reach a wide stony track.

Turn right along the track and pass farm buildings on your left. Good views unfold in front of you. You may see kestrels hovering above the field edges or, if you happen to be walking at dusk or dawn, you could see a barn owl hunting along the ditches. Follow the path as it curves slightly to the left, where a curious little flower garden can be seen on the right of the path. At this point, ignore an unmarked track off to the left, but bear very slightly right and then continue ahead along the main path. A small drainage ditch to the left runs parallel with the path as you go forward. Pass farm buildings to your right and then carry on until you reach a road.

Turn right along the road and pass a house on your right-hand side. Ignore a road immediately on the left and keep going straight on, passing another house on your right. Follow the road as it curves gently to the right, before crossing

Drive and Stroll

over a drainage ditch. Continue along the road, paying careful attention to any oncoming traffic as you go. Further ahead, the road curves slightly to the right as you pass houses on your left. Soon after, pass an attractive farmhouse on your left and then follow the road round to the right and left. Pass a pretty pond and follow the road as it curves to the left, where you arrive at the **Ship Inn**.

Mute swans are among some of the

 (4)

Stay on the road as it bends sharply to the right and then continue, passing the pub on your right. After about 200 yards, step off the road to the left and follow the signed path which takes you along the raised bank of the **Old Bedford River**.

Continue in the same direction as before, now with the river on your left and the road running parallel on your right. As you walk, the birdwatching hides at the edge of the reserve can be seen on the opposite riverbank and there are good views across the landscape to your right. Continue for about 850 yards then walk down the grassy bank to return to the reserve car park.

Place of Interest Nearby

Chatteris Museum is situated approximately 5 miles to the west of the reserve. It tells the history of the area and its people, and a variety of changing exhibitions include natural science, archaeology and social science. There are also archives and old photographs. Open on Thursday afternoons and Saturday mornings throughout the year. Telephone: 01354 696319.

8 | Abbots Ripton

The delightful church of St Andrew in Abbots Ripton

The Walk 3 miles ⏱ 1½ hours
Map OS Landranger 142 Peterborough (GR 233779)

How to get there

From Huntingdon, drive north-east on the A141. After 3 miles, turn left along the B1090, which brings you into Abbots Ripton. **Parking**: Roadside parking is available on Moat Lane.

Drive and Stroll

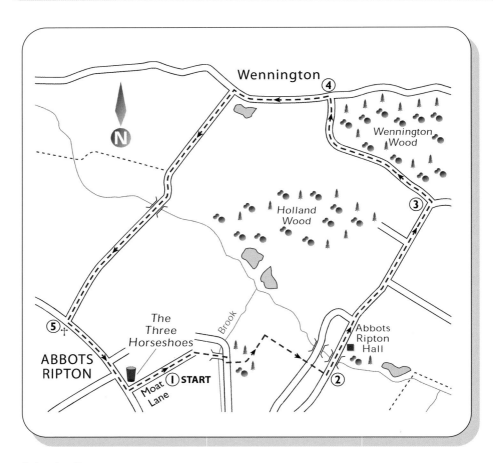

Introduction

This short but enjoyable route starts at Abbots Ripton – an attractive little village situated a short distance to the north of Huntingdon. It boasts thatched cottages, an ancient and beautiful church, a thriving post office and an excellent pub. The surrounding countryside is a mosaic of woodland and arable farmland, and a pretty brook runs nearby. Soon after setting off, you pass a moated house which, at one time, may have been the local manor house. You then come to 18th-century Abbots Ripton Hall. In summer, the landscaped gardens are open to the public. After walking beside the edge of Wennington Wood, you pass through Wennington itself, which is one of the most picturesque villages in the area. A winding country lane then leads you back to the starting point.

Refreshments

The **Three Horseshoes** pub can be found near the start of the route. A wide choice of quality food is available, from bar snacks through to main meals. Real ales are also served and accommodation is available too. Open every day except Monday. Telephone: 01487 733440.

THE WALK

Park on the grassy area at the side of **Moat Lane** and walk away from the pub, passing houses on your left. Shortly after go through a small wooden gate on your right and then walk ahead across a grassy field. To your left, you can catch a glimpse of a beautiful moated house. At the far side of the field, cross a footbridge over a stream and, immediately, another bridge over a drainage ditch. Turn right along a well-surfaced lane and, after a few steps, turn left to go through a small wooden gate. Continue ahead through a small patch of woodland and, at the far side of the wood, turn left to follow a yellow marker arrow. Walk ahead, keeping the wood to your left and a grassy field to your right. At the far side of the field, a yellow marker arrow guides you to the right. Further on, cross a narrow estate lane and go through a kissing gate. Bear slightly left across a grassy field and then go through another gate. After a few steps, go through a kissing gate, to arrive at a gravel track.

Turn left along the track and cross a bridge spanning a brook. A little further on, you pass **Abbots Ripton Hall** on your right, which was used as a hospital during the First World War. Continue ahead, as the gravel track becomes a well-surfaced estate lane. Pass **Hall Farmhouse** on your right and keep going along the lane. Further on, ignore lanes off to your right and left, but keep straight on until the lane branches into two.

Take the left-hand branch, keeping the edge of **Wennington Wood** to your right and a field to your left. Ignore an unmarked path to your right, but keep straight ahead. As you walk, there are good views all around. Follow the lane as it bends round to the right and keep going until you reach a country road.

Turn left along the road and continue into the village of **Wennington**, where you pass picture-postcard cottages and a traditional duck pond. Turn left at a T-junction in the centre of the village

Drive and Stroll

The lane on the edge of Wennington Wood

and then continue along a country lane. Further on, you walk down a gentle incline, where there are good views ahead of you. Ignore a signed path to your right, but continue along the road as it curves first left and then right. Cross a road bridge over a brook and then continue ahead until you reach a junction with the **B1090**.

 (5)

Turn left and walk along the pavement, passing **St Andrew's church** and the post office. Pass **Rectory Lane** on your right and, on reaching the **Three Horseshoes pub**, turn left along **Moat Lane** to return to the starting point.

Place of Interest Nearby

Abbots Ripton Hall is passed near the start of the route. This attractive 18th-century property has wonderful landscaped gardens, which contain rare and attractive trees, roses, herbaceous borders, architectural features and a beautiful lake. The gardens are open to the public on selected Sundays throughout the summer. Telephone: 01487 773555.

9 Prickwillow

The Prickwillow Drainage Engine Museum is housed in the centre of the village

The Walk 5 miles 🕐 2½ hours
Map OS Landranger 143 Ely & Wisbech (GR 597825)

How to get there

Prickwillow is situated on the B1382, 3½ miles to the north-east of Ely.
Parking: Roadside parking is available on Padnal Bank, at the junction with the B1382, close to the church.

Drive and Stroll

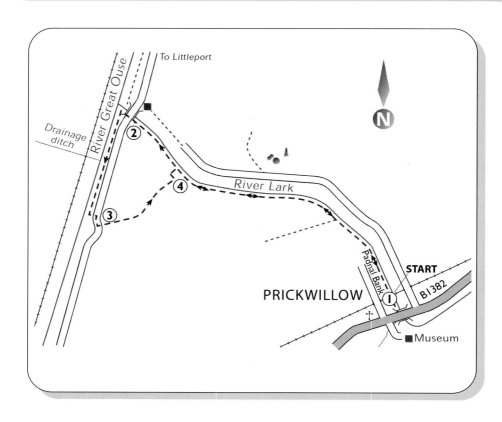

Introduction

This attractive waterside walk starts in the hamlet of Prickwillow which, despite its small size, has an impressive church and a museum. The area was once open fen, consisting largely of reed and osier beds, and it was here that people came to cut prickets, or skewers of willow – hence the name. After the course of the River Lark was changed in 1829, the village was able to develop more fully, with houses being constructed on the firm silt of the old riverbed. Nowadays, the River Lark is still a prominent feature, and the first section of the route takes you along its west bank. As you walk on the raised grassy paths, there are some fine views across the countryside and, in spring, newly arrived swallows can be seen skimming across the surface of the water. The route continues beside the River Great Ouse and then along farm tracks, before the River Lark accompanies you again on the return stretch of the journey.

Refreshments

Prickwillow Drainage Engine Museum at the start of the route provides a limited range of snacks, including tea, coffee and cakes. Telephone: 01353 688360.

For more substantial meals, try the **Black Horse** pub at Littleport, 1¼ miles to the north of Point 2 of the route. Sandwiches are available, as well as dishes such as steak and kidney pie and fish and chips. A beer garden backs onto the River Great Ouse. Open throughout the week. No food all day on Tuesdays, or on Sunday evenings. Telephone: 01353 860328.

THE WALK

At **Padnal Bank** walk along a grassy footpath, keeping the **River Lark** to your right and houses to your left. As you walk along the bank, **Ely Cathedral** can be seen in the distance over to your left. Cross a railway line with care and then go through a gap in the bushes ahead of you. Climb over a wooden fence immediately afterwards and then continue ahead on the raised grassy riverbank. Pass farm buildings to your left and, a little further ahead, pass a marked path on your left. Continue, as the path bends to the left. This part of the river is a good place to see swans and attractive great-crested grebes. Pass under power lines further ahead and continue past a wide track to your left. Immediately afterwards, you pass boat moorings to your right and a house to your left. Carry on along the riverbank and cross a stile, to arrive at a road bridge, which spans the **River Lark** to your right.

Cross the road with care and, on the other side, descend a grassy bank, which brings you to a junction of the **River Lark** and the **River Great Ouse**. Turn left here, to walk along a grassy path with the **River Great Ouse** to your right. As you continue along the raised bank, **Ely Cathedral** can be seen again, this time to your half-right. Carry on along the riverbank, which runs parallel with a road to your left. There are good views for miles around as you walk ahead. Pass a drainage ditch, which runs into the river on the opposite bank, and keep going straight ahead. Just before reaching a small cluster of houses on your left, turn left and descend the grassy bank to leave the footpath. Cross a road carefully and then turn right. After a few yards, you reach a signed footpath.

Turn left to follow the footpath,

Drive and Stroll

which takes you along a stony track and past farm buildings to your right. As the path curves to the left, there are good views across open farmland. After passing a wide, unmarked track to your left, follow the footpath as it curves gently to the right. As you continue, the path can be muddy in places, particularly after heavy rainfall. A little further ahead, you pass a narrow drainage ditch, which can be seen to your right. Soon after, you reach a junction of unmarked tracks.

The path beside the west bank of the River Lark

 (4)

Turn left here and, after about 70 yards, go over a stile on your right-hand side. After climbing up a grassy bank, you will see the boat moorings which were encountered earlier. Turn right and enjoy the riverside views for a second time, this time keeping the water to your left. Follow the grassy path used before and, further on, cross the railway line again. Keep going straight ahead to return to the starting point.

Place of Interest Nearby

Prickwillow Drainage Engine Museum, opposite the starting point of the route, was originally a pumping station. Built in 1880, it was used to pump water from the fields into the river. It now houses several restored pumping engines that date back to the early 20th century. They can be seen working on special 'run-days' held throughout the year. There are also artefacts, photos and documents explaining fenland history. Opening times may vary. Closed from November to March, except for 'run-days'. Telephone: 01353 688360.

10 Catworth

A peaceful scene near Catworth

The Walk 3¼ miles 🕐 1¾ hours
Map OS Landranger 153 Bedford & Huntingdon (GR 085732)

How to get there

Catworth is located on the B660, 9½ miles to the west of Huntingdon, and can be accessed from the A14. **Parking**: On High Street, outside the Racehorse Inn, or patrons may use their adjacent car park.

Drive and Stroll

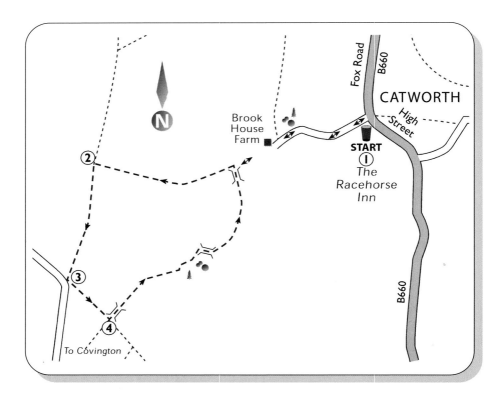

Introduction

Catworth is a pretty little village in the west of the county. It has an olde-worlde village sign sited on a miniature green, a traditional village shop and an adult population of around 300. An ideal starting place then, for a peaceful walk in the countryside. The route begins at the Racehorse Inn and then leads you along a quiet country lane. Soon after, you follow a bridleway beside a shallow brook and continue across rolling farmland to higher ground, from where there are far-reaching views across the rural landscape. You then pass open fields and hedgerows, before walking beside the brook once more and along the country lane that takes you back to the inn.

Refreshments

The **Racehorse Inn** is a multi-roomed pub, with a separate dining area. Real ales are available and a wide choice of food includes snacks such as sandwiches and soup, through to main meals like fish and chips, beef stroganoff, and chicken with garlic and white wine sauce. Vegetarian dishes are always available and traditional roasts are served on Sundays. Open seven days a week. Telephone: 01832 710123.

THE WALK

With the inn behind you, turn left and walk away from **High Street** along a well-surfaced lane, passing farm buildings on your left. A little further on, the lane takes you down a gentle incline and curves first to the right, then the left. As the ground levels out, you pass a small stand of trees to your right – home to a dozen or so pairs of rooks during the breeding season. Ignore a footpath off to the right, and continue past **Brook House Farm**. Go through a wooden gate and continue ahead on a stony track. After about 100 yards, the track bends sharply to the right. Just before this, veer slightly to the left and continue along a grassy bridleway, where a shallow brook accompanies you to your left. Soon after passing a footbridge and a marked path to your left, you reach a junction of tracks. Turn left here and, after a few steps, turn right and walk along a stony path. This takes you up a gentle incline, with fields on either side of you. As the ground steepens, the stony path becomes a grassy track. The ground eventually levels and you reach a T-junction of unmarked paths.

Turn left here and walk along a grassy path, keeping a hedge to your right. As you walk along the ridge, there are excellent views in all directions. Continue along the grassy path, which curves slightly left and right as you go. Immediately after going through a wooden gate further ahead, you will see a narrow lane in front of you.

Turn left here, to follow a signed bridleway. Continue ahead, keeping a ditch and a hedge to your left and fields on either side of you. Soon after passing an unmarked track to your right, you reach a footbridge on the left.

Turn left and cross the bridge, then continue ahead along the edge of a field, keeping a ditch and a hedge immediately to your left. After about 200 yards, follow the path as it curves round to the right and then continue ahead, still with a ditch and a hedge to your left. Walk down a slight incline and, on reaching a wooden marker post, follow a yellow arrow, which guides you to the left. After a few steps, turn right along a stony track, from where there are

Drive and Stroll

good views towards **Catworth**. Follow the track as it bends to the left, then turn right and cross a footbridge. Once across the bridge, bear diagonally left to follow a yellow arrow. The path takes you across a field and then curves to the left slightly, taking you down a gentle slope. At the far edge of the field, cross a footbridge, which was seen earlier on the route, then turn right to walk along the grassy bridleway already encountered. Further on, continue along the lane and pass **Brook House Farm** once more, before retracing your steps back to the **Racehorse Inn**.

Place of Interest Nearby

Hamerton Zoo Park is located 6½ miles to the north-east of Catworth. Set in 15 acres of attractive parkland, it is home to over 100 species of rare and beautiful animals from around the world, including cheetahs, meerkats, snakes, birds and primates. Open all year round. Telephone: 01832 293362.

11 | Grafham Water

Grafham Water is one of the largest reservoirs in England

The Walk 4½ miles ⏱ 2¼ hours
Map OS Landranger 153 Bedford & Huntingdon (GR 166680)

How to get there

From Huntingdon, head west on the A14 for 2½ miles, then south on the A1. On the outskirts of Buckden, head west on the B661 and, after a mile, turn right along an unclassified road. Continue for ¾ mile to reach a car park on your left. **Parking**: Marlow pay-and-display car park, on the eastern shore of Grafham Water.

Drive and Stroll

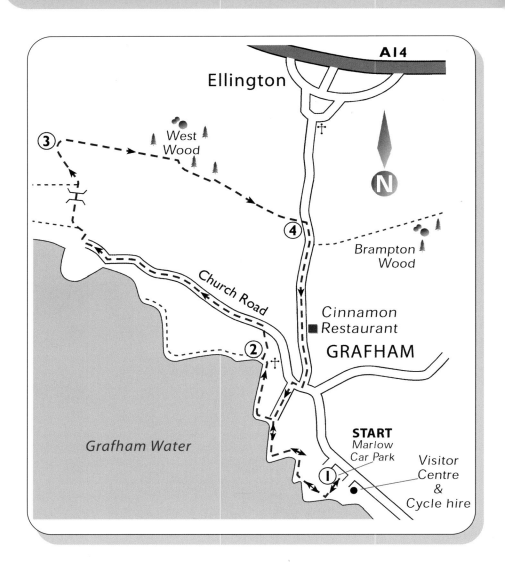

Introduction

This scenic walk starts and finishes on the eastern shore of Grafham Water. It was constructed in the 1960s to supply water to the then new town of Milton Keynes, and to meet the demand of rapidly expanding towns within Bedfordshire and Northamptonshire. Officially opened in 1966 by HRH

Prince Philip, it was originally called Diddington Reservoir, after the little brook that still flows nearby. This man-made lake covers 1,500 acres and is owned by Anglian Water, which encourages leisure use both on and around the reservoir. After walking along grassy waterside paths, the route takes you through farmland and along a country lane, before you loop round past woodland and along a stretch of the Three Shires Way. The return leg of the journey leads you through Grafham village and then back beside the water's edge to the starting point.

Refreshments

Grafham Water Visitor Centre also houses a café. Food includes jacket potatoes, omelettes, and fish and chips. It is open from 11 am to 4 pm on Monday to Friday, and 11 am to 5 pm on Saturday and Sunday. Hours may vary during winter. Telephone: 01480 812154.

Or you may like to try the **Cinnamon restaurant**, which is passed after Point 4 of the route. They serve authentic Indian cuisine throughout the week, from 12 noon to 2.30 pm and 6 pm to 11 pm. Telephone: 01480 812211.

THE WALK

Park facing the water, with the **Visitor Centre** and cycle-hire centre over to your left and a children's playground in front of you. Walk to the right of the children's playground and go along a stony path for about 50 yards. At a junction of tracks, turn right along a stony path, keeping the water to your left. Pass a small stand of trees to your left and then follow the path as it bends to the right and then the left. As you continue, you will see the car park to your right. Follow the main path and, as it takes you close to a road, bear round to the left and go through a metal gate, to follow a signed footpath (also used as part of the cycle route around the reservoir). After passing a wood on your left, veer slightly left and follow a well-trodden grassy path towards the water, then bear slightly right and continue along the path, with the water immediately to your left. As you walk along the shoreline, there are some fantastic views across the reservoir. At a junction of paths further on, ignore a lane off to your right, but keep straight ahead to walk beside the water. After about 400 yards, you reach an inlet with a small stony beach.

Turn right here, along an unmarked, but well-trodden path. This takes you away from the water and past a

Grafham church is passed at point 2 of the walk

stand of trees to your right. At an unmarked junction of paths further on, go through a gap in the hedge in front of you, then walk ahead up a gentle incline. At the top of the incline, bear diagonally left across a field, passing **Grafham church** over to your right. At the end of the field, go left along **Church Road**. Pass a farm complex to your left and then follow the road as it curves to the right. Where the metalled road runs out, follow a stony byway, as it curves to the right then the left.

Ignore a gate and a marked path in front of you, and follow the main track round to the right. Pass under a disused railway bridge and follow the path, as it curves to the left. Ignore a signed bridleway on your left, but continue ahead on a grassy path. Keep a hedge to your right and continue until you reach a wooden marker post.

Turn right here, to follow the **Three Shires Way**. Keep a hedge to your left and then walk along the edge of **West Wood**. Further on, ignore a marked path to your right, and continue along the edge of the wood. At the end of **West Wood**, follow a blue arrow, which guides you to the left, then turn right along a stony track. As you continue,

there are good views to your left. Walk on until you reach a road.

Turn right and walk along the road, keeping alert to any oncoming traffic. As you enter the outskirts of **Grafham** village, you pass the **Cinnamon restaurant** on your left. At a road junction further ahead, turn right along **Church Road** and then turn left along **Church Hill**. At the end of this lane, go through a wooden gate and walk straight ahead. At the edge of the reservoir, turn left and walk along the grassy path, which was used near the start of the walk. Continue, with the water to your right, and retrace your earlier steps past the wood, through the metal gate and then back along the stony path to the car park.

Place of Interest Nearby

The Cromwell Museum is located at Huntingdon, 6¼ miles to the north-east of the starting point of the route. Oliver Cromwell was born in Huntingdon in 1599, and in 1653 he became Lord Protector, head of a British republic. The museum is housed in the building of an old school, which Cromwell himself once attended. There are interesting documents, coins, books and paintings relating to Cromwell. Admission is free. Telephone: 01480 375830.

12 Fen Drayton

The start of the walk

The Walk 5 miles ⏱ 2½ hours
Map OS Landranger 154 Cambridge & Newmarket (GR 339690)

How to get there

From St Ives, drive south on the A1096. After 2½ miles, head south-east on the A14, then, after 3½ miles, turn left along an unclassified road into Fen Drayton. Head for the northern end of High Street and continue as it becomes a wide track (Holywell Ferry Road/byway). **Parking**: Use the free car park off the track, near the gravel pits.

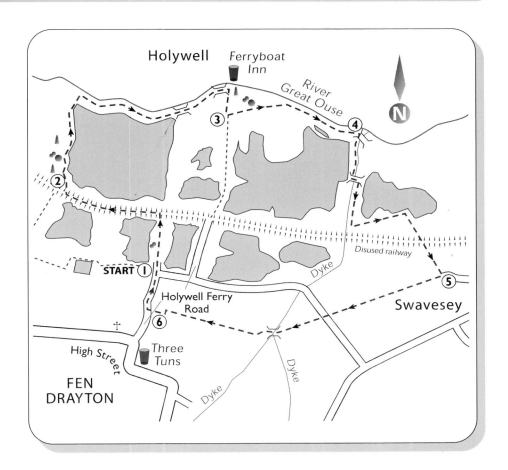

Introduction

This enjoyable route starts on the edge of Fen Drayton – an attractive rural village located about 9 miles north-west of Cambridge. Soon after setting off from the starting point, paths and tracks lead you through a complex of gravel pits, which have been transformed into a series of beautiful lakes. Part of the complex has been designated as a nature reserve, and it is one of the best places in the county for birdwatching – with a large number of species being recorded each year. Later, you walk beside a scenic stretch of the River Great Ouse, where the village of Holywell can be glimpsed beyond the riverbank. After strolling beside a fenland drainage dyke, lanes and paths wind through the countryside and return you to the start.

Drive and Stroll

Refreshments

The **Three Tuns**, on High Street, is an attractive old pub serving a wide choice of food, including snacks such as jacket potatoes and hot baguettes, through to main meals like steak, mushroom and Guinness pie, or home-made lasagne. Real ales are also served. Open all week. Telephone: 01954 230242.

THE WALK

Leave the car park and turn immediately left along a grassy bridleway. As you walk, you will see a drainage ditch and a lake to your right, and a line of trees that hides a lake to your left. After about 650 yards, you arrive at a junction of tracks, with a well-surfaced lane running from left to right which traces the line of a disused railway. Cross to the other side of the lane and then turn left along a grassy bridleway. Continue ahead, keeping a large lake to your right and the lane to your left. After about 750 yards, you reach a corner of the lake, where a line of trees can be seen in front of you.

At this point, turn right along a signed bridleway, still with the lake immediately to your right. Continue on the path until you see the **River Great Ouse** in front of you, then turn right along a path. Keep going, with the lake to your right and the river over to your left. Continue beside the riverbank and follow the path, as it curves first to the left and then the right. Further on, there are good views, as you pass the village of **Holywell** beyond the far bank of the river. Cross a footbridge over a stream and then continue ahead along the main path. Keep going until you see the **Ferryboat Inn** on the opposite riverbank. Cross a footbridge and then turn right along a wide, unmarked track. After about 200 yards, you reach a stile on your left-hand side.

Climb over the stile and walk ahead, to follow a signed footpath. Keep a line of small trees to your left and pass lakes to your right. Further on, the river can again be seen to your left, as the path curves to the right and takes you along a slightly raised bank. Go over a stile and keep going along the main path, where there are fine views in all directions. Further ahead, the path curves sharply to the left and right, as you pass a narrow finger of water to your right. Keep going until you reach a footbridge spanning a drainage dyke, which flows into the river to your left.

Houghton Mill is a working watermill, and well worth visiting

  ④

Do not cross the bridge, but turn right along a grassy path, keeping the dyke immediately to your left. A little further on, you pass lakes on either side of you. Turn left to cross a footbridge spanning the dyke and, on the far side, turn right. After about 150 yards, turn left along a wide stony track. Soon after the track bends to the right, cross the line of a disused railway and continue along the stony track until you reach a sharp bend in a lane.

  ⑤

At this point, turn right to follow a signed path. Continue on this stony track, passing **Friesland Farm** on your right, and a disused windmill – now a kennel and cattery – on your left. Cross a narrow lane and go over a stile on the opposite side, then continue ahead along a grassy path. Cross a footbridge over a dyke and then drop down a shallow bank. Bear slightly left along an unmarked, but well-trodden path. After about 40 yards, follow the path as it curves to the right, taking you across a field. Pass to the side of a metal gate and pass a farm to your left. The path takes you between two lines of trees and curves to the left and right. Cross a footbridge over a ditch to arrive at a wide track (the byway used earlier to access the car park).

Turn right along the track. Further on, ignore an unmarked byway to your right, but continue ahead. Pass a signed footpath to your left and then walk on for a few yards, to return to the car park.

Places of Interest Nearby

The **Norris Museum** can be found at St Ives, approximately 3 miles north-west of Fen Drayton. Founded by St Ivian, Herbert Norris, it tells the story of the historic county of Huntingdonshire, from early times to the present day. Open all year round. Telephone: 01480 497314.

   Houghton Mill (National Trust) is an 18th-century timber-built watermill, located about 4 miles north-west of Fen Drayton. Telephone: 01480 301494.

13 Aldreth

The River Great Ouse

The Walk 4¼ miles 🕐 2 hours
Map OS Landranger 154 Cambridge & Newmarket (GR 445733)

How to get there

From Haddenham, drive south-west for 1½ miles along an unclassified road, which takes you through Aldreth village. **Parking**: Roadside parking is available at the far end of High Street.

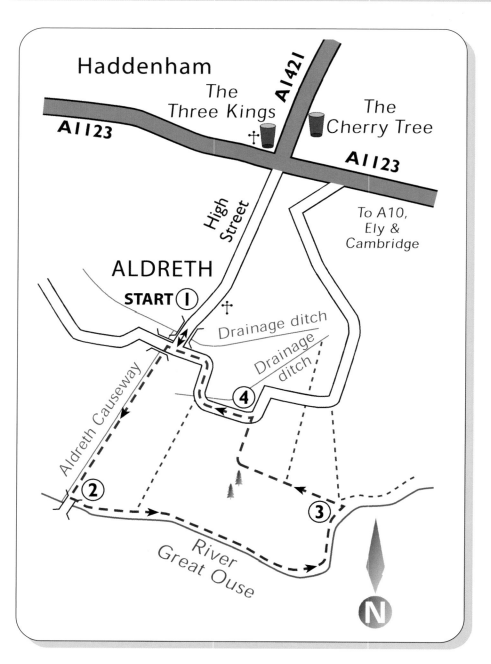

Introduction

The sleepy village of Aldreth hides a fascinating and turbulent past, for it was once the site of violent clashes between William the Conqueror and the renowned Saxon leader known as Hereward the Wake. In the 11th century, Aldreth stood at the southern tip of the Isle of Ely – an area of raised ground surrounded by water, swamps and marshland. Hereward and his men took refuge here and, using their local knowledge, they were able to find ways across the marshes to attack the invading Normans, before retreating back into the swamps. William built a timber causeway across the marshes, but when his army tried to cross, it collapsed under the weight of their armour and chain mail. Soon after, it is said that the monks of Ely showed William a secret way onto the Isle, so ending Saxon resistance. Hereward evaded capture, however, and slipped out of the history books and into legend. The first leg of this route takes you along Aldreth Causeway, which follows the same route as the one built by William the Conqueror all those years ago. Later, you walk beside a beautiful stretch of the River Great Ouse, before paths and country lanes guide you back to the start.

Refreshments

The **Three Kings** at Haddenham, 1½ miles north-east of Aldreth, has a reputation for good food, and serves snacks such as sandwiches, through to main meals like chicken breast stuffed with spinach, in a white wine and cream sauce. It is open all day throughout the week, though no food is served all day Monday or on Sunday evening. Telephone: 01353 749080.

Alternatively, try the **Cherry Tree**, which serves a variety of real ales and traditional pub food such as fish and chips, and steak and ale pie. Open all day on Friday, Saturday and Sunday, and closed between 3 pm and 6 pm during the rest of the week. Telephone: 01353 740667.

THE WALK

At the bottom of **High Street**, cross a bridge over a drainage ditch and walk straight on. Cross a narrow lane and continue ahead on a signed path, following the route of **Aldreth Causeway**. In recent years, Norman swords and timbers have been found in this vicinity. As you continue on the wide, grassy path, you will notice a raised bank to your right, beyond which is a drainage ditch. Walk ahead, where there are good views to your left. Pass disused barns to your right and, just before reaching a bridge, you will see a wooden kissing gate on your left-hand side.

Drive and Stroll

A short drive away is the impressive Ely Cathedral

2

Go through the gate and walk ahead along a well-trodden path, keeping the River Great Ouse to your right. Further on, ignore a wide, unmarked track to your left, but go through a kissing gate and continue ahead. On the opposite bank of the river, you pass **Smithey Fen Engine** – an electric pumping station used to control water levels. Go over a stile and continue along this picturesque stretch of river. In spring and summer, the grassy banks are covered with colourful wild flowers, and a variety of birds can be seen. Further on, go over two stiles in quick succession and then follow the path as it curves to the left, running parallel with the course of the river. The path then bends to the right slightly.

 ③

Immediately before reaching a sharp right-hand bend in the river, turn left and walk down a grassy bank, before going through a metal gate. Continue ahead on a wide, grassy path, where there are good views to your right. Further on, ignore a wide, unmarked track to your right, but keep straight ahead on the main path, which can be muddy in places. Over to your left, you will be able to see the raised riverside banks that you walked along a few moments ago. As you reach a line of old trees on your left-hand side, follow the path as it bends sharply to the right. Enjoy the views as you walk ahead and continue until you reach a bend in a narrow lane.

 ④

Turn left along the lane, which is said to have been built by prisoners during the Second World War in order to allow food supplies to be transported into the area. Further on, a wide drainage ditch to the right runs parallel with the lane. Follow the lane as it bends sharply to the right and then cross a bridge over the drainage ditch. Walk ahead and then follow the lane round to the left, passing farm buildings to your left and houses to your right. A little further ahead, you will see **Aldreth Causeway** to your left, which was encountered at the beginning of the walk. At this point, turn right and cross the bridge over the drainage ditch, then walk a short distance along **High Street** and back to the starting point.

Place of Interest Nearby

The historic and attractive city of **Ely** is located 7½ miles to the north-east of Aldreth. It boasts a magnificent Norman cathedral, which is well worth a look, and you can also visit the house where Oliver Cromwell and his family lived between 1636–1647 (also home to the Tourist Information Centre). Telephone: 01353 662062.

14 Wicken Fen

The confluence of Reach and Burwell lodes

The Walk 4¼ miles ⏱ 2 hours
Map OS Landranger 154 Cambridge & Newmarket (GR 564706)

How to get there

From Ely, head south on the A10 for 3 miles, then drive south-east on the A1123 for 4 miles. On reaching Wicken village, turn right along Lode Lane. **Parking**: Use the National Trust car park at the end of Lode Lane. Although parking is free, donations are encouraged.

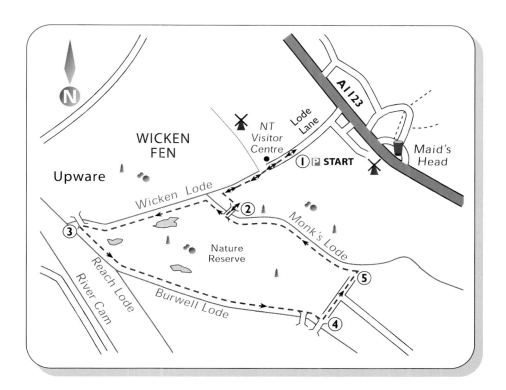

Introduction

This satisfying circuit takes you around Wicken Fen – the National Trust's oldest nature reserve. Since the first purchase of land back in 1899, a continuous programme of acquisitions has seen the fen develop into one of the most important wetland reserves in western Europe, supporting a wide variety of rare birds, insects, mammals and flowers. It is also a beautiful area in which to walk, and this route takes advantage of a network of well-marked footpaths, which will lead you beside peaceful waterways, reedbeds, sedge fields and traditional fenland scenery.

Refreshments

The National Trust visitor centre and café are located close to the car park. Drinks and ice creams are available at the visitor centre, while sandwiches, soup, light lunches, drinks and cakes are served at the café. Opening times may vary, particularly during winter. Telephone: 01353 720274.

Drive and Stroll

Alternatively, you may wish to try the **Maid's Head**, in the centre of the village. They serve a wide choice of food, including sandwiches, daily specials, bar snacks and more substantial meals. Real ales are also available. Open seven days a week, closed at lunchtime on Tuesdays. Telephone: 01353 720727.

THE WALK

Leave the car park and turn left along the lane, passing houses to your right. A little further on, pass **Fen Cottage** on your left. Owned by the National Trust, it was restored in the late 1980s using raw materials from the fen. Soon you pass the National Trust visitor centre and café over to your right. The lane ends at this point and the route continues ahead on a signed footpath. Carry on along the grassy path, keeping **Wicken Lode** to your right. As you walk, you can see a wind pump over to your right. Follow the path as it curves round to the right and, at a junction of waterways, turn left along the path and continue to a footbridge.

Cross the footbridge over the water and then turn right. Follow the path round to the left and then continue ahead, still with **Wicken Lode** to your right. After about 150 yards, go through a gap in a wooden fence and walk straight on, passing a birdwatching hide to your left. Further on, you pass the mere – a series of pools over to your left. In summer, this is a good area to see marsh harriers drifting overhead. These rare and spectacular birds of prey sometimes breed on the reserve. Continue ahead, passing a tower hide on the opposite bank of the lode. Further on, go through a gap in a wooden fence and carry on along the main path, still with the clear water of the lode to your right. Go through a wooden gate beside a stile and follow the path, as it curves gently to the right and then the left. Keep going until you reach a wooden footbridge on your right.

You may like to stand on the raised bridge to enjoy good views across the countryside before you turn left and climb over a stile, then walk ahead on a grassy path. Continue, now with **Reach Lode** to your right. Further on, you come to a confluence of waterways. **Reach Lode** branches off to the right, but the route continues ahead, beside **Burwell Lode**. Pass a pool over to your left and, soon after, follow the path as it curves gently to the left. Further on, climb over a wooden fence and then pass a bridge spanning **Burwell Lode**. After about 40 yards, you reach another bridge.

The windpump at Wicken Fen

Drive and Stroll

4

At this point, turn left along a stony track, which soon becomes a well-surfaced lane. Pass open fields to your right and farm buildings to your left. Ignore a road off to the right, but keep straight ahead, where the lane soon becomes a stony track once more. Further on, ignore a path off to the right, but go through a small wooden gate and continue ahead on a stony path. Keep going until you reach a raised grassy bank in front of you.

5

Turn left here and go through a gate, before continuing along the path, keeping **Monk's Lode** to your right. Follow the course of the lode, as it bends gently to the right and then the left. Pass through a gap in a wooden fence and continue ahead. A little further on, turn right to cross the footbridge used earlier. Turn left at the far side of the bridge and then follow the path round to the right, retracing your earlier steps beside **Wicken Lode**. Pass the visitor centre and café, then continue to the car park.

Places of Interest Nearby

The **National Trust Visitor Centre** houses interesting information and leaflets about the fen and its history, guided walks, maps, books and nature sightings. Tickets and access to Fen Cottage and the windpump are obtainable from the centre. Opening times may vary. Telephone: 01353 720274.

Anglesey Abbey and **Lode Mill** (both National Trust) are located 6¼ miles to the south of the fen. The abbey was built on the site of a 12th-century Augustinian priory, and attractions include fine paintings, silver, furniture and tapestries, as well as beautiful gardens. The nearby mill is open to the public for milling demonstrations. Times may vary. Telephone: 01223 810080.

15 Abbotsley

The village green in Abbotsley

The Walk 4 miles 🕐 2 hours
Map OS Landranger 153 Bedford & Huntingdon (GR 227565)

How to get there

From St Neots, head roughly south-east on the B1046. After about 4 miles, you reach Abbotsley. **Parking**: Patrons may use the car park at the Jolly Abbot, which overlooks the village green. Otherwise, park on the roadside nearby.

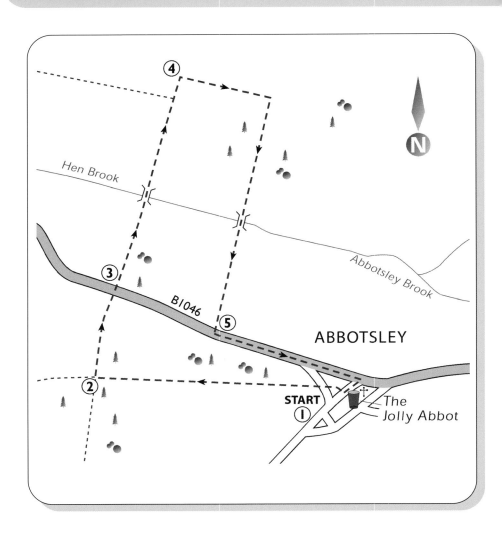

Introduction

Situated close to the historic market town of St Neots, the charming village of Abbotsley boasts thatched cottages, an ancient church and a friendly community atmosphere. This enjoyable route starts and finishes at the Jolly Abbot pub, which stands beside the attractive village green. Along the way, there are beautiful views to enjoy, as you walk through farmland dotted with woodland and copses, and pass a pretty brook and a moated house, before a well-surfaced footpath returns you to the starting point. The route is particularly enjoyable in early summer, when wild roses can be seen in the hedgerows.

Refreshments

The **Jolly Abbot** is a welcoming village pub, with a large open plan bar and a separate eating area. A wide range of food is served throughout, and includes light snacks, as well as more substantial meals. Topnot real ale is brewed especially for the pub by Potton Brewery. Open seven days a week. Food is served every day except Monday. Telephone: 01767 677765.

THE WALK

With the main entrance of the pub behind you, turn left along the road. Follow it round to the left, then turn right to walk across the village green. Cross a narrow road and then walk straight ahead along **Hardwick Lane**. At the edge of a park, a yellow arrow guides you straight on. At the far side of the park, follow another yellow arrow, which guides you ahead again. Continue up a gentle incline, keeping a hedge to your left. As the ground levels, there are good views to the right. At the far side of the field, follow a marker arrow straight ahead and pass a stand of trees to your right. The path takes you down a gentle slope, before the ground levels out again. Continue, with a hedge to your left. Walk up a slope and, near the end of the field, follow a marker arrow through a short

stretch of woodland, to reach a junction of paths.

At this point, turn right along a grassy bridleway, keeping a hedge to your left and the wood to your right. Where the wood ends, keep straight ahead, still with the hedge to your left. Between the gaps, you can glimpse a golf course. A little further on, the grassy path becomes a stony track, which curves slightly to the right before dropping downhill. Good views unfold ahead of you. Continue until you reach the **B1046**.

Cross the road with care and then follow the signed byway on the opposite side. Continue straight ahead on the wide, grassy track, passing a wood to your right. A little further on, the path takes you over a brook, before curving to the left slightly. Keep to the main path

On the route at point 3

and, further ahead, follow it round to the left and up a gentle incline. Ignore a marked path to the left but continue until you reach a marker post.

  (4)

Turn right here, keeping a hedge to your right and open fields to your left. Further ahead, the path becomes a little wider, and there are excellent views all around. Continue ahead and then turn right along an unmarked, but well-surfaced path, which takes you through a farm complex. Pass a barn to your left, then veer slightly right and pass a large brick building to your left. Immediately after, pass to the right of a metal gate and follow a yellow arrow, which guides you slightly to the right. Pass an impressive moated house to your left and then continue ahead on a well-surfaced farm lane, which takes you down a gentle incline. As you walk, there are trees over to your left and right, and good views ahead. Follow the lane as it curves to the left, taking you past an attractive house. The path then curves to the right, taking you over **Abbotsley Brook**.

Continue along the lane until you reach the **B1046**.

Cross the road and then turn left along the pavement, passing houses to your right and left. Continue ahead, passing beautiful thatched cottages on your left and the village green to your right. From here, you return to the **Jolly Abbot** pub over to your right.

Place of Interest Nearby

St Neots Museum, 4 miles to the north-west of Abbotsley, is situated close to the east bank of the River Great Ouse in the same building as the Tourist Information Centre. This lively museum tells the story of the market town of St Neots, from prehistoric times to the present day. Opened in 1995, the wide array of exhibits includes pottery, costumes, sporting trophies and even the leg bone of a woolly mammoth. There are interactive displays for children. Open from February to December. Times may vary. Telephone: 01480 214163.

16 Great Eversden

Heading back to Great Eversden

The Walk 4 miles ⏱ 2 hours
Map OS Landranger 153 Bedford & Huntingdon (GR 227565)

How to get there

From Cambridge, head south-west on the A603 for 5½ miles, then turn right along an unclassified road into Great Eversden. **Parking**: Roadside parking is available at the end of Wimpole Road. Take care not to obstruct driveways.

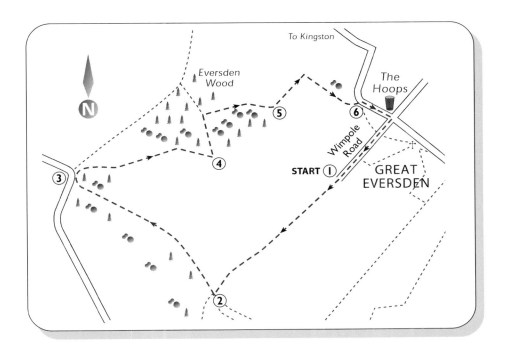

Introduction

Great Eversden is an ancient and attractive village, set amid beautiful countryside. Eversden derives from the word 'Eversdona', which can be found in the Domesday Book, and which means 'hill of the wild boar'. In 1466, the village church was badly damaged by fire, after it was struck by lightning. It was then rebuilt in the late 15th century, and underwent restorations in 1846 and 1920.

The first leg of this route takes you up a gentle incline to higher ground, from where there are excellent views behind you towards Cambridge. Grassy paths then lead you through rural farmland and mature woodland, before you walk through village streets and back to the starting point.

Refreshments

The **Hoops** is located in the centre of the village and is passed on the route. It specialises in quality Thai cuisine. Sandwiches, light snacks and traditional Sunday roasts are also available, as well as a wide choice of dishes from a regularly changing specials board. Open seven days a week. Telephone: 01223 264008.

THE WALK

From the roadside, walk away from the village centre, passing farm buildings to your right and an attractive thatched house to your left. Immediately afterwards, ignore a signed footpath on your right, but continue along a wide, stony bridleway. The track curves slightly to the right, before taking you up a gentle slope. After passing open fields on either side of you, the ground begins to level out. If you look behind at this point, there are good views across the countryside and, on a clear day, you can see the city of Cambridge in the distance. Continue ahead on the bridleway, with **Eversden Wood** visible over to your right. After the path curves to the left slightly, you arrive at a junction of tracks.

Turn right here, to follow a signed bridleway. This takes you along a wide, grassy track and past two water storage buildings on your right-hand side. As you continue, keep a line of trees to your left and open fields to your right. A little further on, follow the path as it curves round to the left. After a while, the path straightens out and you reach the edge of a wood in front of you. At this point, go straight ahead along an unmarked, but well-trodden path through the wood. Soon after, ignore an unmarked path off to the left, but walk ahead until you reach a bend in a lane.

Turn right along the lane and, after a few steps, turn right along a signed footpath. Ignore a path off to the left, but continue ahead, keeping the wood immediately to your right. Follow the path as it curves gently to the right and continue until you reach the far side of the wood. At this point, bear diagonally left on an unmarked path across a field. At the far side of the field, a yellow arrow on a marker post guides you to the right. Continue on a wide path, with **Eversden Wood** to your left and a line of trees to your right. After about 220 yards, you reach another marker post on your left-hand side.

Turn left here and walk along a grassy path, which takes you through **Eversden Wood**. Turn right after about 200 yards, to follow another grassy path through the wood. In spring, bluebells and other wild flowers make this area particularly attractive. A little further on, ignore an unmarked track to the left and continue ahead. On reaching the edge of the wood, ignore a grassy ride to your right, but walk straight on, keeping a field to the left and another section of woodland to the right. Follow the path as it curves to the right and drops downhill. As you reach the end of the woodland to your right, you arrive at a marker post.

(5)

Follow the yellow arrow, which guides you round to the left. Continue, passing fields immediately to your left and with a drainage ditch to your right. As you walk, there are good views ahead. After about 750 yards, a track in front of you runs from left to right. Turn right here and pass a small marker post and a hedge on your left. The path takes you up a gentle slope, with fields on either side of you. The ground then levels, before taking you down a gentle incline. At the bottom of the slope, go over a stile beside a gate and then bear very slightly right. Follow a well-trodden path across a meadow and pass an old solitary tree on your left. Soon after, pass farm buildings to your left and then follow the path as it curves to the left. Go over a stile and pass to the side of a gate, which brings you to a bend in a road.

The magnificent 18th-century Wimpole Hall

 (6)

Turn right along the road and continue, passing attractive beamed cottages as you go. Further on, you reach a crossroads, where the **Hoops** pub can be seen to the left. Either pop in for refreshments, or turn right along **Wimpole Road**. Continue along the road passing more attractive houses, before returning to the starting point.

Places of Interest Nearby

Wimpole Hall and **Wimpole Home Farm** (both National Trust) are located 2½ miles to the south-west of Great Eversden. The magnificent 18th-century hall is set in scenic parkland, while the farm is home to rare animal breeds. Telephone: 01223 206000.

17 Lode

Lode Mill

The Walk 3½ miles 🕐 1¾ hours
Map OS Landranger 154 Cambridge & Newmarket (GR 531627)

How to get there

Lode is situated 5½ miles north-east of Cambridge city centre, and is accessible from the B1102. **Parking**: Roadside parking is possible near the end of Mill Road, off High Street.

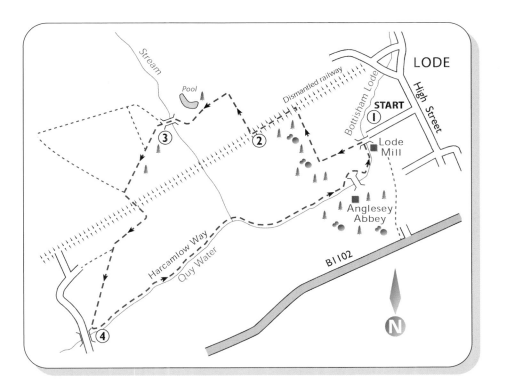

Introduction

Lode, formerly known as Bottisham Lode, lies in a peaceful and picturesque setting on the edge of the Cambridgeshire fens. This walk begins close to an attractive 18th-century watermill, which, like nearby Anglesey Abbey, is owned and managed by the National Trust. In 1982, the Cambridgeshire Wind and Watermill Society completed a restoration of the mill, and it is now one of the few working, water-powered, flour mills in Britain. After passing the mill, there are open fields and woodland to enjoy. Later, you cross a bridge over a crystal-clear stream and then pass through lush green meadows, before the return leg of the journey leads you along a stretch of the Harcamlow Way, beside the banks of Quy Water.

Refreshments

Nearby **Anglesey Abbey** offers a wide range of food, including a children's menu, in its licensed restaurant. The abbey can be reached by footpaths running from the mill near the start of the route, or by car, off the B1102 to the south-west of Lode. Opening hours may vary. Telephone: 01223 810080.

Alternatively, the **White Swan** at Stow cum Quy is situated about 750 yards from Point 4 of the route. Sandwiches through to steaks are available, alongside a good choice of real ales. No food on Mondays. Telephone: 01223 811821.

THE WALK

Walk to the end of **Mill Road** until you reach **Lode Mill**, then turn right and cross a footbridge at the point where **Quy Water**, to your left, meets **Bottisham Lode** to your right. Lodes are drainage ditches, many of which were built during Roman times. Once across the bridge, follow the signed path straight ahead. As you continue, the path curves slightly to the left. On reaching the edge of a wood, turn right, keeping a hedge to your right-hand side. At the end of the hedge, a white arrow on a marker post guides you to the left. Continue on a wide track (dismantled railway), passing the wood to your left and open fields to your right. Soon after, you reach a wooden marker post by a track on your right-hand side.

Turn right along this grassy track. In spring, the hawthorn trees on either side of the path are covered in pretty blossom. Look out also for rabbits running across the path in front of you. At the end of the path, turn left along a wide track, which can be very muddy after heavy rainfall. As you reach the edge of a field further on, walk straight ahead, to follow a yellow arrow on a marker post. Over to your right you can see reeds and trees, which hide a small pool. Follow the clearly defined track as it bends to the right, taking you along the edge of a field.

At the far side of the field, cross a footbridge over a clear shallow stream and then bear diagonally left to follow a path marked '**Quy**'. After about 10 yards, bear left again and continue through beautiful green meadows. If you walk here in spring and early summer, you will be able to see a variety of wild flowers. Go over a stile and continue ahead, following marker posts as you go. At the far side of the meadow, go through a kissing gate on your left and then bear slightly right, to follow a track marked '**Quy**'. At a junction of paths further on, turn left along a wide, stony track. Further ahead, cross a wide path (dismantled railway) and continue. After about 100 yards, follow the track as it bends to the right, from where there are good views all around. Continue for about 650 yards, then bear diagonally left to go through a kissing gate and across a grassy field. Continue until you reach a gate and a wooden fence beside a lane.

If, at this point, you want to visit the **White Swan** pub for refreshments, turn left and walk along the lane for about 750 yards. Otherwise, turn sharp left to walk along the **Harcamlow Way**, keeping **Quy Water** immediately to your right. Go through a metal kissing gate and continue along the grassy path, as it curves gently to follow the water course. A stand of trees on the far bank conceals the grounds of **Anglesey Abbey**. Follow the path as it curves to the right, still with **Quy Water** to your right. As you continue, you may be lucky enough to see a kingfisher darting by. Further on, you will see a footbridge to your right and the grounds of the

Green meadows abound on this walk

abbey beyond. At this point, follow a yellow marker arrow, which guides you to the left. After a few steps, bear right again and then continue ahead, with **Quy Water** to your right. After passing large poplar trees, follow the path, as it curves gently to the left. Continue past **Lode Mill**, immediately to your right, to arrive back at **Mill Road**. The signed paths on the opposite side of the road will lead you to **Anglesey Abbey** after about 650 yards. Alternatively, turn left along the road to return to the starting point.

Places of Interest Nearby

Lode Mill is passed on the route and **Anglesey Abbey** is located nearby. (See Walk 14 for details.)

18 Abington Pigotts

The walk begins by skirting a strip of woodland

The Walk 3¾ miles ⏱ 2 hours
Map OS Landranger 153 Bedford & Huntingdon (GR 307445)

How to get there

Abington Pigotts is located 4¼ miles to the north-west of Royston, and is sandwiched between the B1042, the A505, the A1198 and the A1. Country lanes which lead to the village can be accessed from these main roads. **Parking**: Park on High Street, near the village hall, or patrons may use the car park of the nearby Pig and Abbot pub.

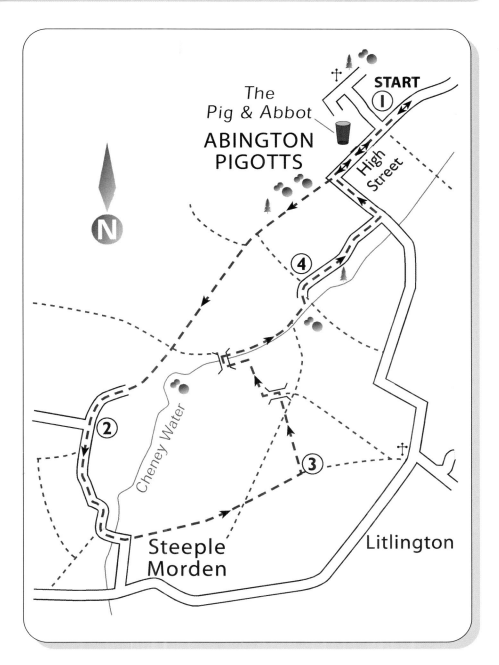

Drive and Stroll

Introduction

The delightful little village of Abington Pigotts lies in the south-west corner of Cambridgeshire, close to the borders of both Hertfordshire and Bedfordshire. Its history can be traced to Norman times, although its origins are thought to date back to the Anglo-Saxon period, or even earlier. This enjoyable route takes you through open farmland and along country lanes, before leading you beside Cheney Water. Towards the end of the walk, you pass a moated farm with an attractive and ancient gatehouse. Quiet roads then guide you through the village and back to the start.

Refreshments

The **Pig and Abbot** pub at the start of the route provides a good choice of quality food. Examples include home-made soup, chilli, steak and kidney pudding, steaks and fish dishes. Real ales are also available. Open throughout the week. Telephone: 01763 853515.

THE WALK

(1)

From the village hall, walk along **High Street** and pass thatched houses, and **Church Lane** on your right-hand side. Soon after, pass the **Pig and Abbot** pub on your right and then continue along **High Street**. At a left-hand bend in the road, bear slightly right, to follow a signed footpath. After passing a house on your left, walk straight ahead, keeping a field to your left and a strip of woodland to your right. Where the wood ends, follow a marker arrow, which guides you straight on. A little further on, the stony path bends to the right. Ignore this, but walk ahead along a grassy path, where views across open farmland can be enjoyed. Pass small wooded areas to your left and ignore tracks off to the left and right. Where the grassy path ends, continue ahead along a lane, passing houses to your right. Follow the lane as it bends to the left and continue to a road junction.

(2)

Take the left-hand fork in the road and pass a house on your right. Pass a signed path on your right and continue along the road, as it bends to the left and then the right. Follow the road round to the left, which takes you down a gentle incline and over **Cheney Water**. Pass **Hillside Farm** on your left and then take the next signed path on your left. This takes you up a gentle slope and along a stony track. As the ground levels, there are sweeping views across the countryside.

The ancient gatehouse and moated farm can be seen towards the end of the walk

Further on, follow a marker arrow on a post, which guides you ahead. After about 200 yards, you reach a marker post at a junction of paths. Continue ahead along the wide track, which soon takes you down a gentle incline, where you arrive at a junction of paths.

 (3)

A wooden pole indicates only the path ahead. At this point, however, turn left along an unmarked grassy path. Soon after, ignore a junction of paths and continue ahead. A little further on, you reach a footbridge on your right. Ignore this, but turn left to follow a yellow marker arrow. After about 40 yards, follow another yellow arrow, which guides you to the right. Walk along the edge of a field, with a drainage ditch to your right. At the corner of the field, turn left and continue until you reach a series of wooden steps on your right. Descend the steps and cross a footbridge spanning **Cheney Water**, then turn right and continue, keeping **Cheney Water** to your right. Further on, pass an unmarked track to your right and continue beside the water. At the far side of a field, walk ahead onto a narrow lane and pass a house to your right. Ignore a signed path to the right, but continue ahead, passing a house to your left. Immediately after, you will see an ancient and impressive gatehouse to your right – this leads to the moated **Down Hall Farm**. Carry on along the lane,

which curves round to the left and brings you to a signed bridleway, slightly to your left.

At this point, bear round to the right and then continue along a narrow road, keeping fields to your left and trees to your right. Turn left at a T-junction and carry on along the road, paying attention to any oncoming traffic. Follow the road as it bends to the right and pass the footpath used near the start of the walk. Pass the **Pig and Abbot** pub on your left and continue ahead for a short distance, where the route ends.

Places of Interest Nearby

Wimpole Hall and **Wimpole Home Farm** (both National Trust) are located about 4 miles to the north of Abington Pigotts, just off the A1198. (See Walk 16 for details.)

19 | Hinxton

The 17th-century Hinxton Mill is passed on the route

The Walk 3 miles ⏱ 1½ hours
Map OS Landranger 154 Cambridge & Newmarket (GR 496451)

How to get there

From Cambridge, head roughly south-east on the A1301. After 8½ miles, turn right into Hinxton and right again along High Street. **Parking**: Park on High Street, near the Red Lion pub (patrons may use their car park).

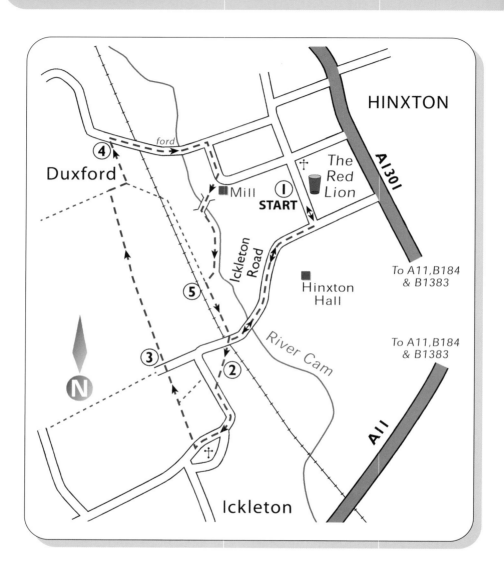

Introduction

This relatively short walk is ideal for all the family, and is particularly enjoyable throughout spring and summer. It begins in the pretty village of Hinxton, with its thatched houses, historic church and attractive pub. Soon after setting off, you pass Hinxton Hall, before lanes and well-marked paths lead you through beautiful countryside. Later, a restored 17th-century watermill is encountered, as you walk beside a tranquil stretch of the River Cam. Grassy paths and quiet lanes then return you to the starting point.

Refreshments

The **Red Lion** can be found on High Street, where a wide range of quality food is served, including snacks like home-made soup, through to main meals such as fillet steak, or pork medallions with apple and calvados sauce. A fine selection of real ales is also available. Open seven days a week. Telephone: 01799 530601.

THE WALK

Walk along the pavement, passing the **Red Lion** pub on your left. At a T-junction, turn right along **Ickleton Road**. As you continue, **Hinxton Hall** can be glimpsed over to your left. This Grade II listed building is now a leading scientific and medical research facility. Carry on along the road, where the **River Cam** can be seen to your right. You may wish to change sides occasionally, in order to keep a clear view of oncoming traffic. Pass a wooden footbridge to your right and, soon after, cross a road bridge spanning the river. Immediately afterwards, go over a level crossing to reach a signed footpath on your left.

Go through a wooden kissing gate on your left and then bear slightly right, to follow the well-trodden path across a grassy field. At the far side

of the field, go through a kissing gate and turn left along **Brookhampton Street**. Walk through the attractive village of **Ickleton** and, on reaching a bend in the road, turn right along **Butcher's Hill**. As you walk up a slight incline, the unusual spire of the village church can be seen to your left. At a left-hand bend in the road, go through a metal kissing gate on your right and then walk ahead along a signed footpath. Go through a kissing gate and continue ahead. At the far side of a grassy field, go through a metal kissing gate and cross a footbridge spanning a ditch. At the far side of the bridge, bear very slightly left. Ignore a marked path to the right, but cross a grassy field. Go through another kissing gate and continue ahead, passing a cemetery over to your right. At the far side of a field, go through a wooden gate, to arrive at a junction of tracks.

Turn right, then immediately left, to follow a signed path towards

Drive and Stroll

The ford where the River Cam crosses the road

Duxford. Carry on along the track, with trees and bushes on either side of you. Walk up a gentle incline and, where the trees and bushes end, go straight ahead along a path that runs parallel with a line of telegraph poles. Where the line ends, go straight ahead across a field. At the far side of the field, go through a gap in a hedge and then turn right.

Continue ahead, keeping the hedge to your right. At the end of the hedgerow, turn left along a grassy path. As the grassy path becomes a stony track, continue ahead and go over a stile to reach a lane.

Turn right along the lane and go over a level crossing soon

afterwards. After about 150 yards, the **River Cam** runs across the road. At this point, you can either walk through a shallow ford, or cross via a bridge. Once across the river, continue ahead along the lane. After about 120 yards, turn right along a narrow lane and, as you reach a sharp left-hand bend, bear right to follow a signed path. Pass a building and then follow the path round to the left. Ahead of you is **Hinxton Mill** – a beautifully restored 17th-century watermill. After passing the mill on your left-hand side, ignore a permissive path in front of you, but bear right to follow a yellow marker arrow. Cross a footbridge and turn left along a path, keeping a wire fence to your right. Go through two narrow gates in quick succession

and continue ahead. Further on, the **River Cam** can be seen to your left. A little further ahead, ignore another permissive path by a gate, but bear right to follow a marker arrow and then continue to a narrow metal gate.

 (5)

Turn left and go through the gate, then continue along a grassy path, which runs parallel with the railway line to your right. At the end of the path, turn left and cross the road bridge spanning the **River Cam**, encountered near the start of the route. Continue along the road and pass **Hinxton Hall** on your right, then turn left along **High Street** and walk the short distance back to the starting point.

Places of Interest Nearby

Hinxton Mill is passed after Point 4 of the route. This restored 17th-century watermill is owned by Cambridge Preservation Society, and is open to the public on National Mills Weekend in May, and on the first Sunday of the month from June to September. Telephone: 01223 243830.

The **Imperial War Museum** is located at Duxford, 2½ miles north-west of Hinxton, by junction 10 of the M11. This is Europe's premier aviation museum, which also houses military vehicles and naval exhibits. Spectacular flying displays take place. Telephone: 01223 835000.

20 Horseheath

The attractive countryside on the Cambridgeshire/Suffolk border

The Walk 3½ miles 🕐 1¾ hours
Map OS Landranger 154 Cambridge & Newmarket (GR 615471)

How to get there

From the centre of Haverhill, drive west along the A1307. After 3½ miles, turn right along a minor road (Haverhill Road) and continue for about 200 yards. **Parking**: Park on Haverhill Road.

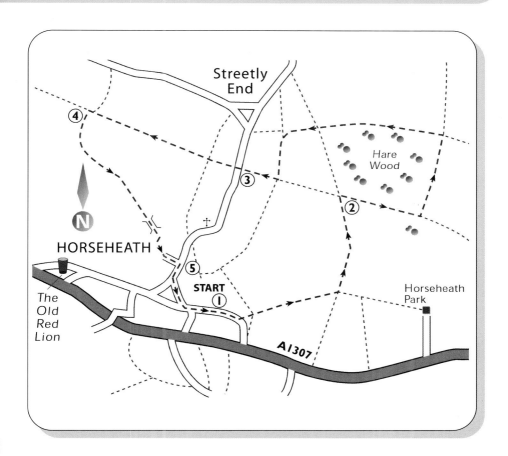

Introduction

The attractive village of Horseheath is situated in south-east Cambridgeshire, about a mile away from the Suffolk county border. It has an ancient church, thatched cottages, a tiny village green and an old inn. At one time, racehorses, including the Derby winner of 1834, were trained at nearby Horseheath Lodge. Despite this, it is thought that the village name has no connection with either horses or heaths. The most likely theory is that it was named after the Horseth family – owners of Horseth Hall, which stood in the area centuries ago. This scenic circuit takes you through the surrounding countryside of gently rolling farmland and woodland, before a pretty brook accompanies you on the homeward leg of the journey.

Drive and Stroll

Refreshments

The **Old Red Lion** on the edge of the village, serves a wide range of good quality food, including snacks and main meals. There is a choice of real ales and a beer garden can be enjoyed in fine weather. Accommodation is also available. Open seven days a week. Telephone: 01223 892909.

THE WALK

From the roadside, walk along the pavement away from the village centre and up a gentle incline, passing houses and cottages on either side of you. As the road begins to curve to the right, bear diagonally left to follow a signed footpath across a field. Ignore unmarked paths to the left and right, but continue ahead. Cross a footbridge over a drainage ditch and then carry on along the path, which runs alongside a line of wooden telegraph poles. After walking up a gentle slope, you reach a junction of marked paths. At this point, turn left along a grassy track, keeping a field to your right and a hedge to your left. Follow the path round to the left, where you pass the grounds of **Horseheath Park** to your right. Soon after, walk across a field until you reach a stony lane.

Turn right along the lane and then pass the edge of **Hare Wood** on your left-hand side. At a junction of unmarked paths, turn left along a grassy track and continue ahead, with the edge of **Hare Wood** to your left and open fields to the right. As you walk, there are good views to your right, towards **Haverhill** and beyond. At the far corner of the wood, turn left along an unmarked path and walk down a slight incline, still with the edge of the wood to your left. Further on, go through a gap in a hedge and continue along the path, as it curves gently to the left. At the corner of the wood, bear very slightly left along a well-trodden path across a field. Go straight on at a junction of unmarked paths and continue to another junction of unmarked paths, where you will see a small wire fence in front of you. At this point, bear round to the left and cross a field, then continue ahead to a stony track. Turn right along the track and carry on until you meet a road.

Cross the road, with care, and then follow the signed bridleway on the opposite side. At a junction of paths further on, continue ahead along the muddy track and keep going as it curves slightly to the left. Carry on along the edge of a field, keeping a hedge to your right. As you walk, there are good views across open

On the way to Hare Wood

countryside. Follow the path down a gentle incline and pass a marked path beside a metal gate on your right. Soon you reach another metal gate on your right.

Turn left here and walk along a grassy path, keeping a narrow brook to your left. Follow the path, as it curves first to the left and then the right. Cross a footbridge at the far side of a grassy field and then go through a wooden kissing gate on your right. Once through the gate, bear left and walk along the edge of a grassy field. At the far side of the field, go through a kissing gate and continue ahead, passing houses to your right. After passing garages on the right, veer slightly right to reach a road. Veer round to the left and continue along the road to reach a T-junction.

Drive and Stroll

Cross the road and then turn right, passing the tiny village green on your right-hand side. At a road junction by the green, turn left along **Haverhill Road**. Pass attractive thatched houses and cottages and then keep going ahead until you return to the starting point.

Place of Interest Nearby

Linton Zoological Gardens can be found 3½ miles to the west of Horseheath. A variety of rare and exotic creatures can be seen, including leopards, lions, tigers, lemurs, owls, parrots and spiders. The park is set in 16 acres of beautiful gardens, with picnic areas, children's play areas, coffee shop and gift shop. Open every day except Christmas Day and Boxing Day. Telephone: 01223 891308.